Automobiles In Tintypes

From the author's collection

Robert W. Caldwell

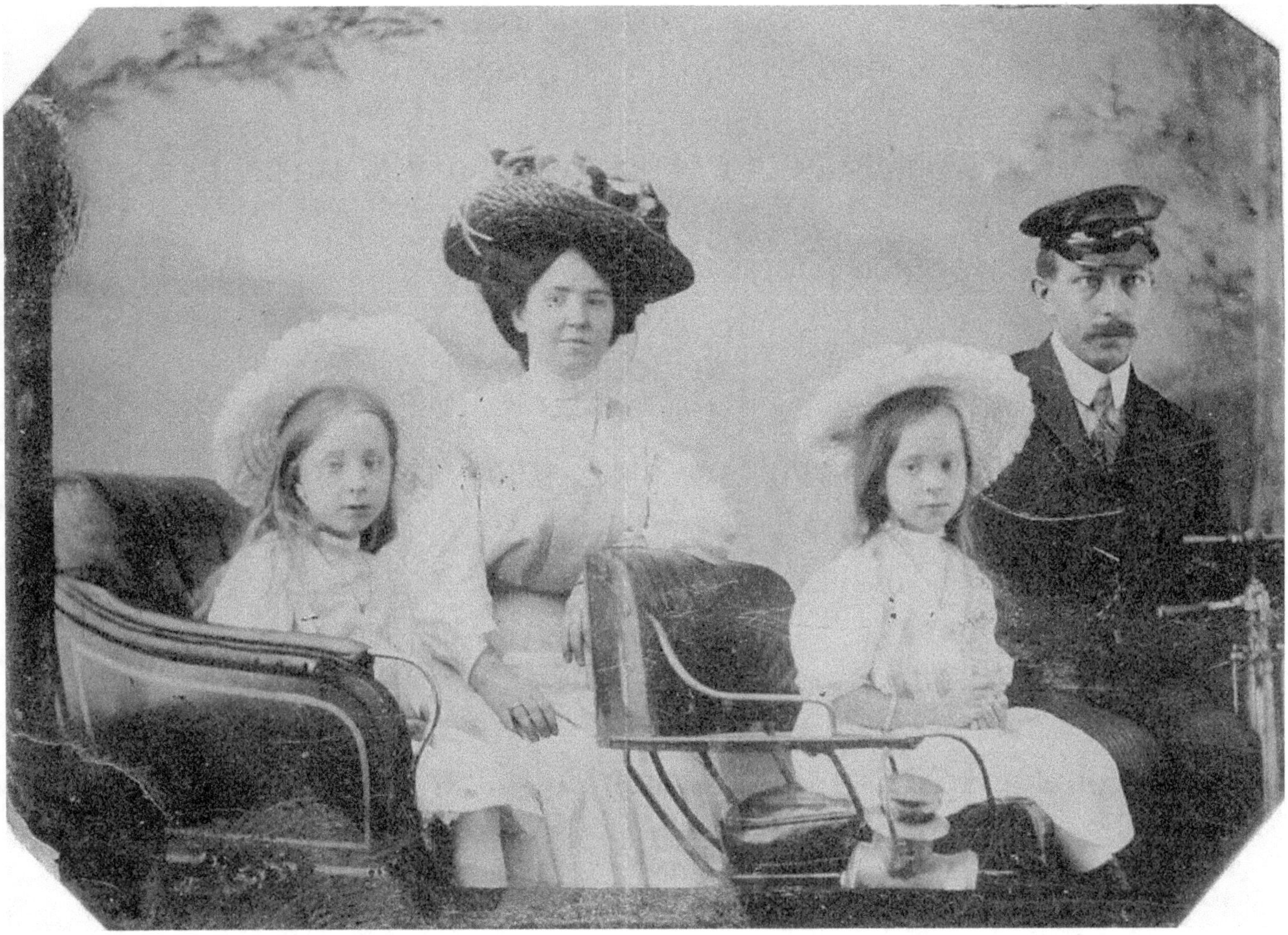

Photography was still a novelty for the lower and middle classes at the turn of the last century as much as automobiles. Both items were desirable. Automobiles were the latest development in technology and people were eager to see them and have their photographs taken in them. Therefore, photographers who owned or had access to a car would stage it in a photo studio or photo booth and charge people to have their photos taken in it.

By the 1880s tintypes were produced at resorts, carnivals, galleries, fairs, and expos. People out for a family stroll along boardwalks, seashores, or other areas would walk into a gallery.[1] "They wore work clothes or came barefooted. They arrived at the door of the photographic studio with their dolls and dogs, trumpets and tools. The props were generally their own..."[2] They would leave with an inexpensive keepsake of the day,[3] one that might include an automobile.

In the Nineteenth Century, the revolutionary invention of photography involved a competition between two different processes the Daguerreotype and the calotype. For a while, the Daguerreotype dominated because of its clarity and brilliance, but improvements on Talbot's method lead to the invention of the collodion process in 1851 by Frederick Scott Archer which used glass plate negatives printed on paper.[4] Tintypes were a variation of this process.

Photography's importance as more than a novelty became firmly established at the 1851 Great Exhibition in London. Here visitors "... saw a massive change in information management: in the creation and dissemination of visually based graphic information characterized by images of the building, its contents and their display... Photography played a crucial role in this quantum leap."[5]

Now we had a visual memory. People became able to see the faces of prominent people and historic people from the past.

Tintypes did not possess the brilliance of daguerreotypes but were popular because they were cheap, easier to make, and durable. Now a greater variety of people had the opportunity to get their portraits made, Civil War soldiers, immigrants, and working-class people. A whole new range of subject matter opened up, including automobiles. Tintypes, for a long time the only form of instant photography, stubbornly hung on, used by sidewalk portraitists at parks, fairs, and beaches, or as a kind of folk art.[6]

As the century mark approached, came, and went, another revolutionary invention came to the starting line; the automobile. Just like with photography multiple technologies raced to become the dominant propulsion system; steam, electric, and gasoline -- and tintypes were there to record it. The earliest automobiles shared unpaved roads with horses and wagons.

The first glimpse many people got of the automobile came at the first American auto show in New York City held at Madison Square Garden on November 3, 1900. 160 different vehicles were displayed. The visitors may have seen the cars as merely a novelty as they watched manufacturers give driving and maneuvering demonstrations on a twenty-foot-wide track that surrounded the exhibits, and as they watched them being driven up a wooden two hundred foot ramp that tested hill-climbing power.

To the 48,000 visitors who paid fifty cents each, gasoline proved to be the least popular source of engine power. "An innovative assortment of electric, steam, and 'internal explosion' engines powered these horseless carriages." The most popular cars proved to be electric, steam, and gasoline, in that order. To show the perils of prophecy one early critic complained that the internal combustion engine was, "Noxious, noisy, unreliable, and elephantine. It vibrates so violently as to loosen one's dentures. The automobile industry will surely burgeon in America, but this motor will not be a factor."[7]

As demonstrated at the show, at first early consumers preferred electric cars because these vehicles were more comfortable and easier to operate. The engine is smaller and lighter than an internal combustion engine. It is also better suited to the speed and torque characteristics of the axle, thus avoiding the need for the heavy and complex transmission required for an internal combustion engine. The steam car is also quieter.[8]

However development of automotive technology proceeded rapidly, due in part to the hundreds of small manufacturers competing for market share. Advances in internal combustion technology; greater range, faster refueling times, and growing petroleum infrastructure, plus mass production which reduced prices led to a decline in the use of electric automobiles.

Jeff Ray at Barber Motor Sports Museum in Birmingham Alabama wasn't a lot of help when I asked for an identification of what kind of car was in a tintype. "The automobile as we know it was not something commonly seen. These vehicles were called 'Horseless carriages' and were built by different individuals or small inventors and were not cookie cutter. The basis of construction was powering an existing design such as a horse carriage... With this understood, I doubt that this can be positively identified."[9] That was a lot of help. Undaunted I am researching and making my best guesses. Some makers were successful, most not.

Among these numerous early automakers were Haynes, Mason, Duesenberg, and Duryea Motor Wagon Company which In 1893 became the first American automobile manufacturer.

Olds's dominated the era with their introduction of the Oldsmobile Curved Dash. Not to be outdone the Thomas B. Jeffery Company followed, developing the world's second mass-produced automobile, the Rambler. Cadillac, Winton, and Ford with the ubiquitous Model T were also producing cars in the thousands. The Studebaker brothers, who transitioned from horse-drawn vehicles to electric automobiles in 1902, and then gasoline in 1904 were also players. Between 1907 and 1912 in the United States, there were over seventy-five makers including Holsman, IHC, Dodge, and Sears which sold by catalog.

A few European automobiles may have found their way into American tintype studios such as the Austro-Hungarian Präsident and the French Renault. Innovation continued rapidly and rampant, with no clear standards for basic vehicle architectures, body styles, construction materials, or controls; for example, many cars used a tiller, rather than a wheel for steering.

In addition, across the northern United States, local mechanics experimented with a wide variety of one-of-a-kind prototypes. But how many of those would end up in a photography studio?

Throughout this period the automobile was seen more as a novelty than as a genuinely useful device. Breakdowns were frequent, fuel was difficult to obtain, roads suitable for traveling were scarce, and rapid innovation meant that a year-old car was nearly worthless.[10]

Perhaps these were passed on to tintypists to be used as props. Automobiles would prove to be as massive a change in transportation as photography was for information.

Now that automobile technology was well underway, the time was opportune for an emerging technology to join with an archaic Nineteenth-Century one. Most I believe were real cars used for photos at amusement areas as it was just simpler and cheaper than building a realistic prop. "By the 1880s tintypes were seldom created with serious portraiture in mind. It was produced at resorts, carnivals, galleries, and other venues... Most likely out for a family stroll, possibly along a boardwalk,... The hats in particular give away the clues that this is an afternoon event,... Tintype galleries along boardwalks, seashores, or other areas that attracted leisure activity provided people with an inexpensive keepsake of the day."[11]

From just before the beginning of the Twentieth Century to 1914 a variety of different automobile designs made their way into these studios, either as is, or modified, as well as car model props made by the tintypists themselves, all of which can make identification difficult. I put horizontal pictures sideways so that you can see them better.

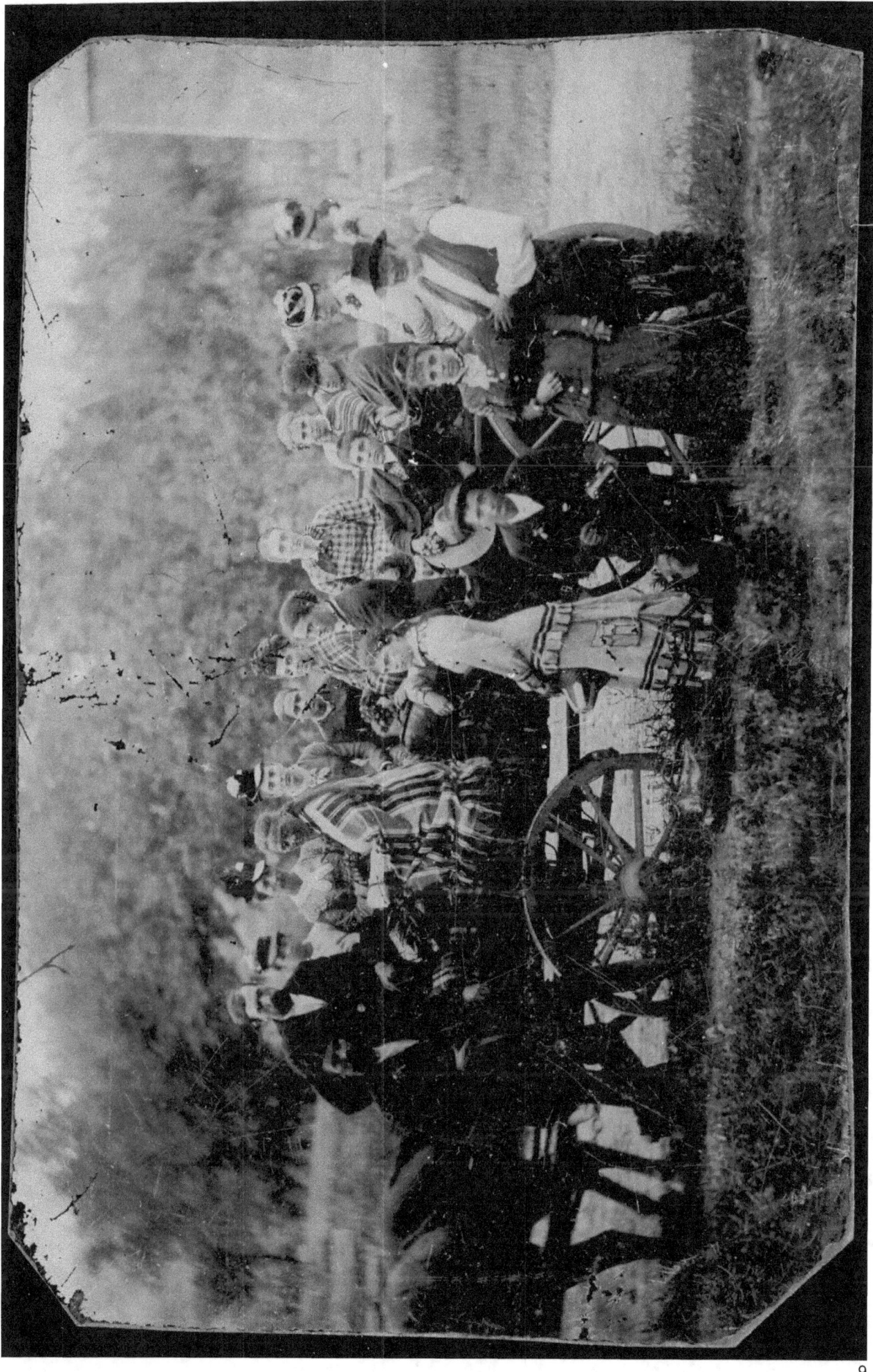

Celebration (But of what?)

This isn't a car but people's fascination with wheeled vehicles goes back as far as the first chariot.

"Hey everybody! Let's do a group picture." Things haven't changed much since those words may have been spoken more than a century ago, except now we would have many pictures of what the group was doing and those pictures would be posted on social media and everyone would be tagged.

At the trade show during 3D-Con in Murfreesboro, Tennessee I was pursuing the tables and met Jeremy Rowe. This tintype jumped out at me so I bought it from him.

This group photo had significance to these nineteen people, but how they related to each other and what the occasion was that is recorded is a mystery to us. Perhaps it was the making of the tintype itself that was the occasion. My interest in collecting is largely based on speculating on the unanswerable questions.

This tintype is about the size of a playing card. Scanning it to a larger image makes it easier to study the details. It was probably taken somewhere in Old West. Based on hair styles, hats and the neck treatments I'd date it to around 1876-78. It has an interesting ratio of three females to each male. We see a variety of different styles of dress.

It looks like there is a creek behind them. A woman wears a shawl that looks Native American made. The girl in plaid in the front holds seems to be holding flowers. The little kid looks like he's holding the same kind of flowers on his hat. Three women in the back look like sisters, two of them might be twins, are dressed similarly and wear hats with a white visor. Two girls in the back of the wagon wear slouch hats highly decorated with flowers. They also have bows on the lapels of their white dresses. The man second from the left in the foreground looks like he is holding a tintype in his hand. Perhaps an early version of this one. I wonder if the camera used made multiple exposures so that more than one person got to keep a copy.

Why is the woman in a light-colored dress, perhaps Native American inspired, holding her hat rather than wearing it like everyone else with a hat except for the child? Why are those four people standing beside the wagon? The man on the far right seems to have some relationship with the woman standing next to him since his hand is clutching her upper arm. Is she his daughter? Or possibly his wife?

The man on the left standing next to the horses is apparently the driver. Obviously, there are more people than the wagon can carry comfortably for any great distance so it is unlikely they were out for a ride, so why is the driver included in the group? The wagon seems to be a prop, possibly owned by the photographer. The tintype included no information about the photographer, so we do not know if the image was taken by a local operator or a traveling photographer.

Like many unidentified images, we will probably never have definite answers to all our questions about the circumstances around their creation. We can just appreciate the images for what they show us and what they might be telling us.

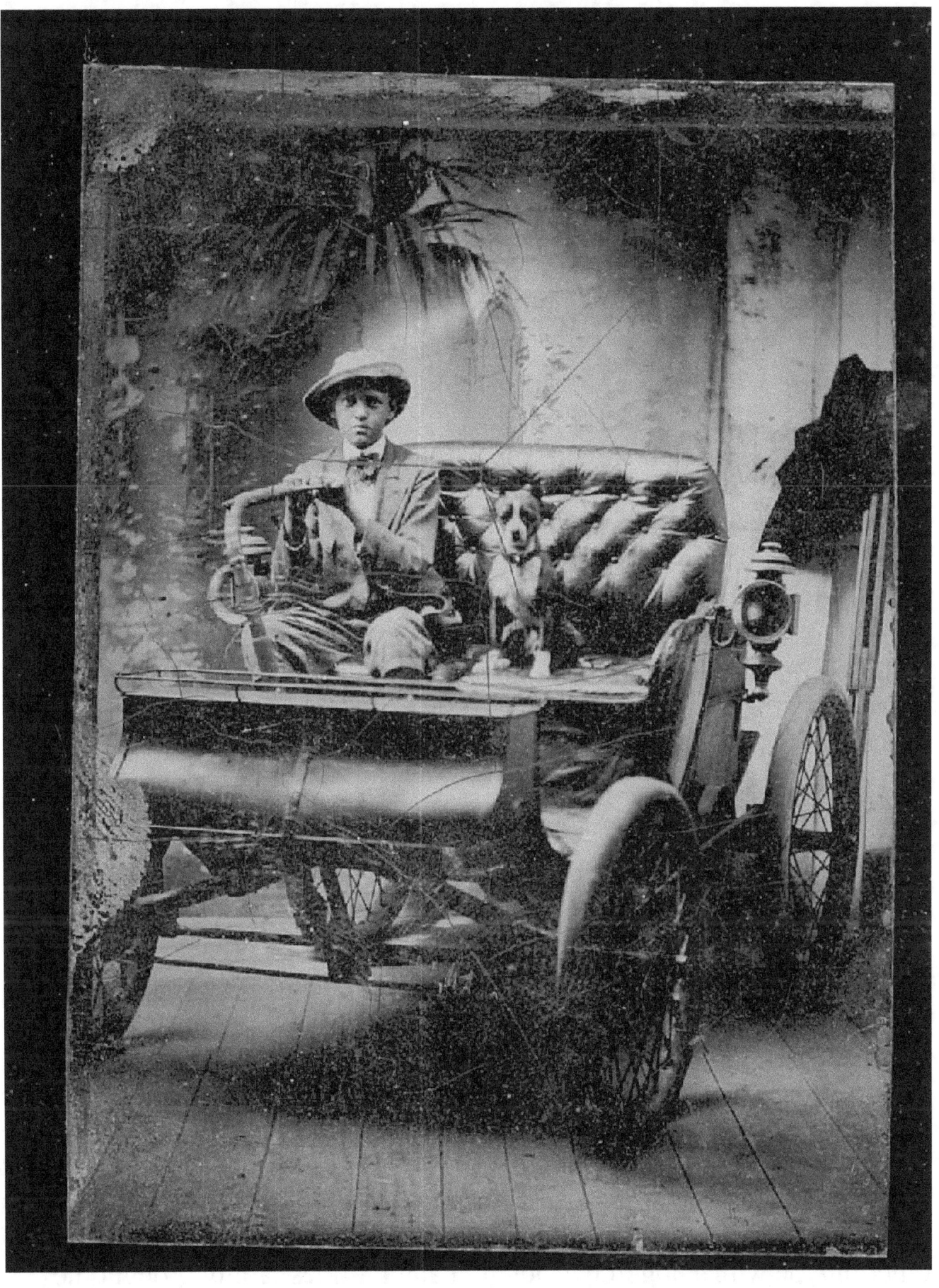

Call the dog, a common photo companion, hop in a two-passenger car that might be a 1903 Oldsmobile Curved Dash and let's head out on a road trip. We fuel up at what must have been a studio; I don't think that people took their dogs to amusement parks. And the tintype has good sharpness and contrast though there is a wavy pattern on the emulsion of half of it.

This car is a runabout with a two-speed transmission, center chain drive, and a mechanical brake. The Curved Dash is credited as being the first mass-produced automobile. It was made from 1901 through 1907. 19,000 were built in all. It would have only cost $650.

Those who are into auto mechanics would be interested in knowing it had a flat-mounted water-cooled single-cylinder engine, which was situated at the center of the car. It produced 5 hp and relied on a brass gravity feed carburetor. The transmission was semi-automatic and had two speeds for forward and one for reverse. The car weighed 850 pounds and had a top speed of a whopping twenty miles per hour.[12]

Dogs seem to be a popular inclusion in tintypes as we see with this other tintype with a dog in it. Though many families family brought the dog with them I wonder if in some cases the animal might have been a

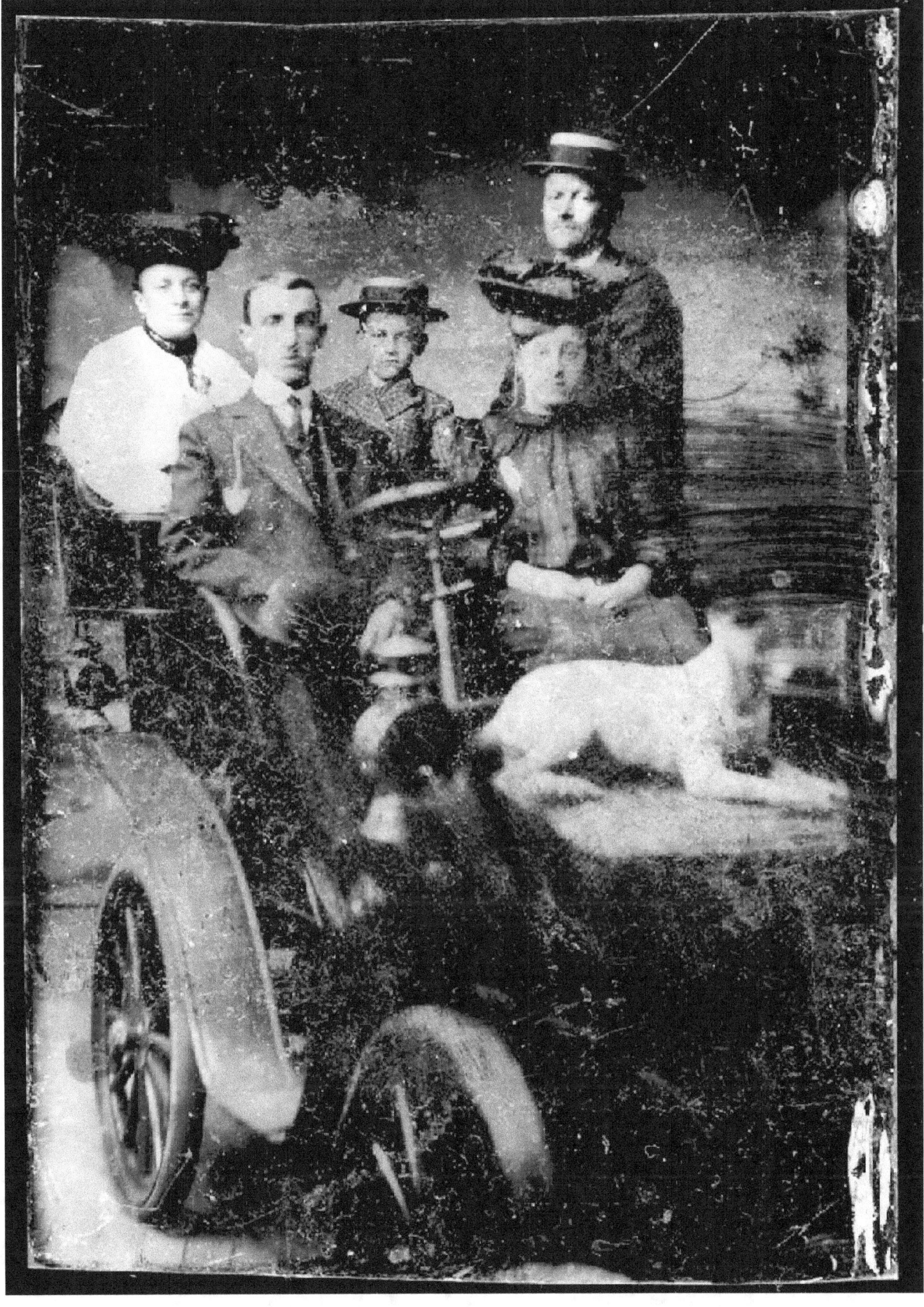

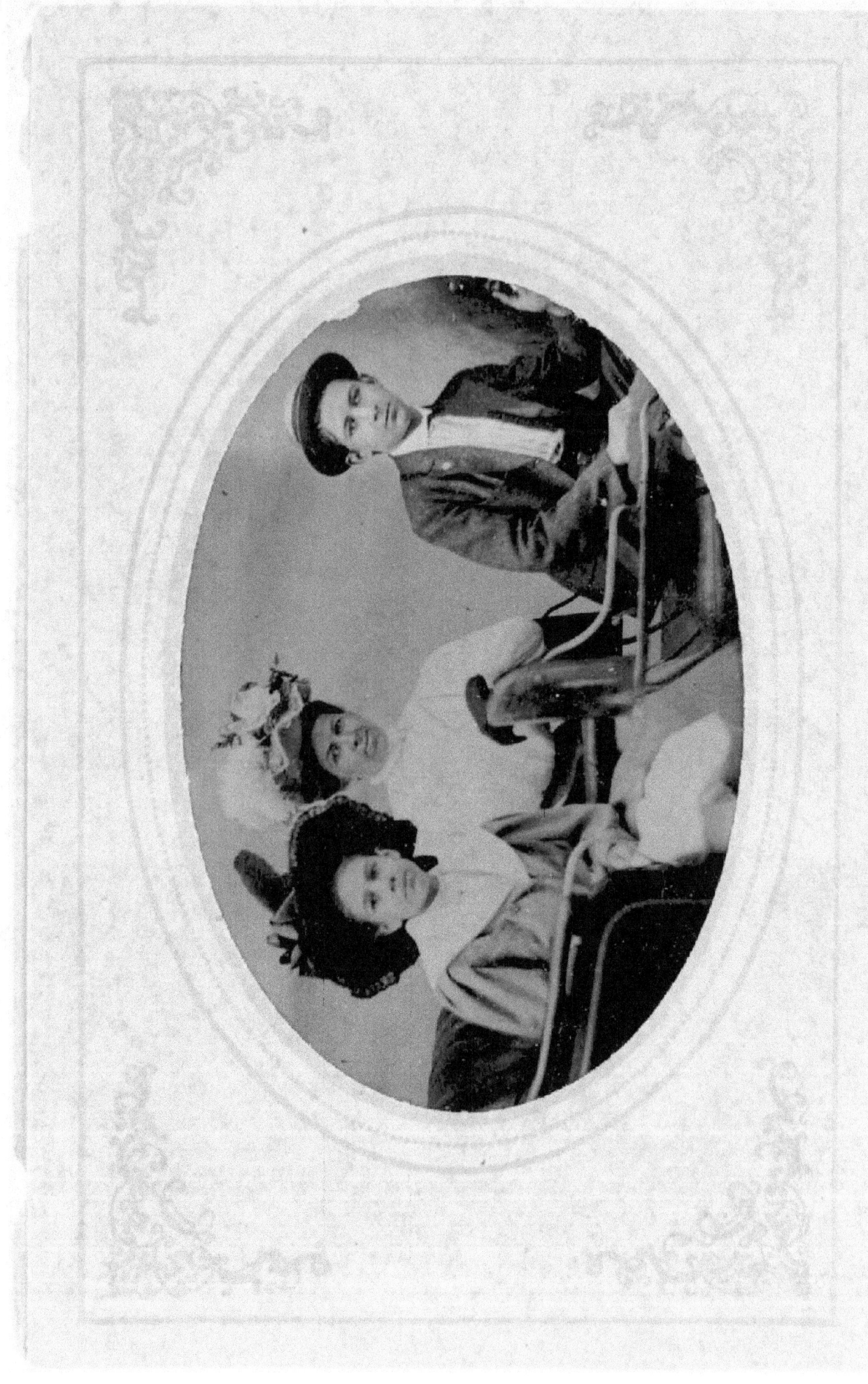

studio dog. A dog could entertain customers and calm down nervous people. Most people would be happy to include the studio dog in their shots. The animal may be sitting comfortably in its favorite spot but forgets to hold still for the exposure. Dogs were such popular subjects that one studio at least had a dog-shaped lamp on the car in a photo I saw on eBay.

Our first stop is Coney Island in 1904 where members of the

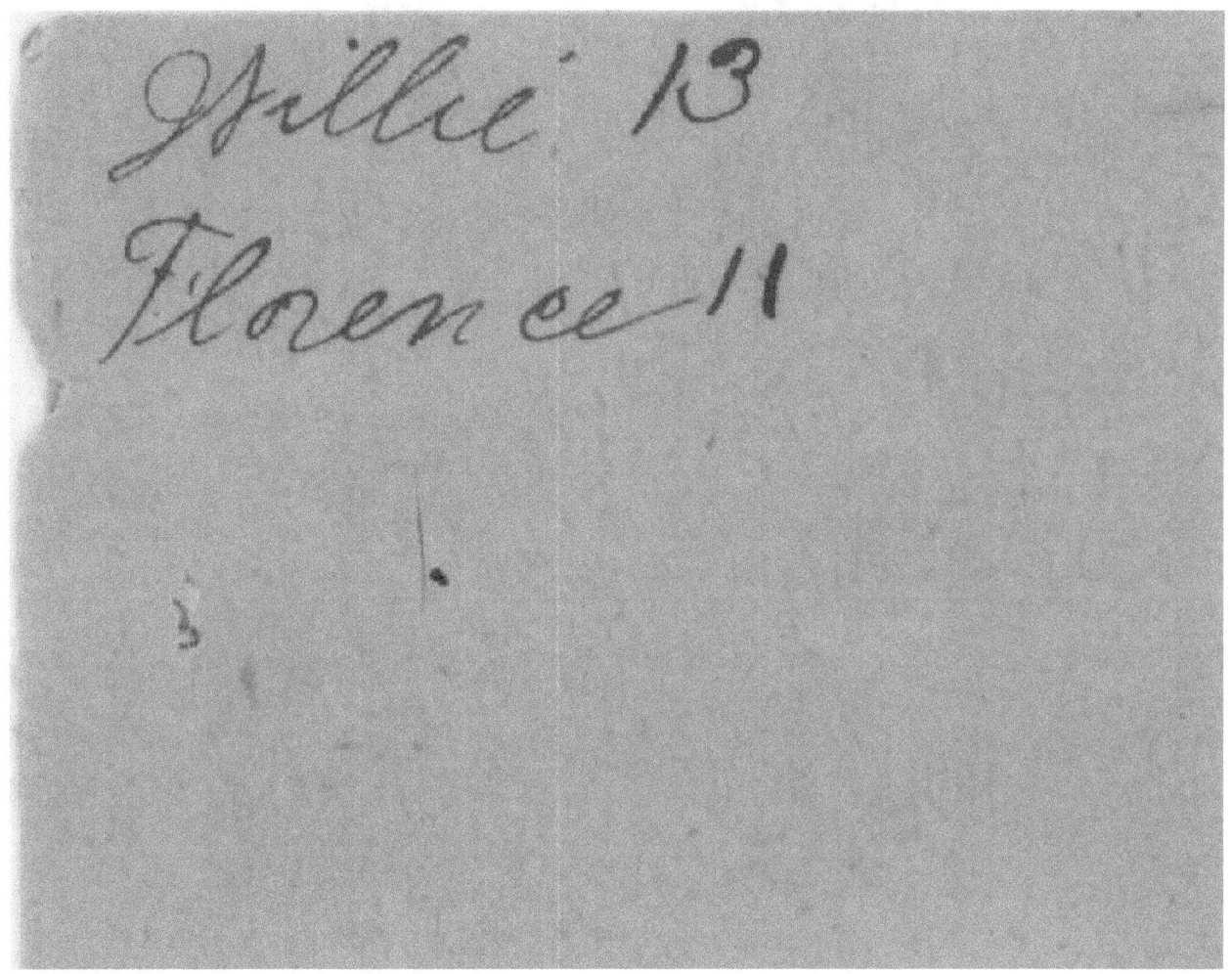

Cobey family walk into the Mammoth Photograph Gallery on Surf Avenue to get their picture made in a prop car. William "Willie" [13] and

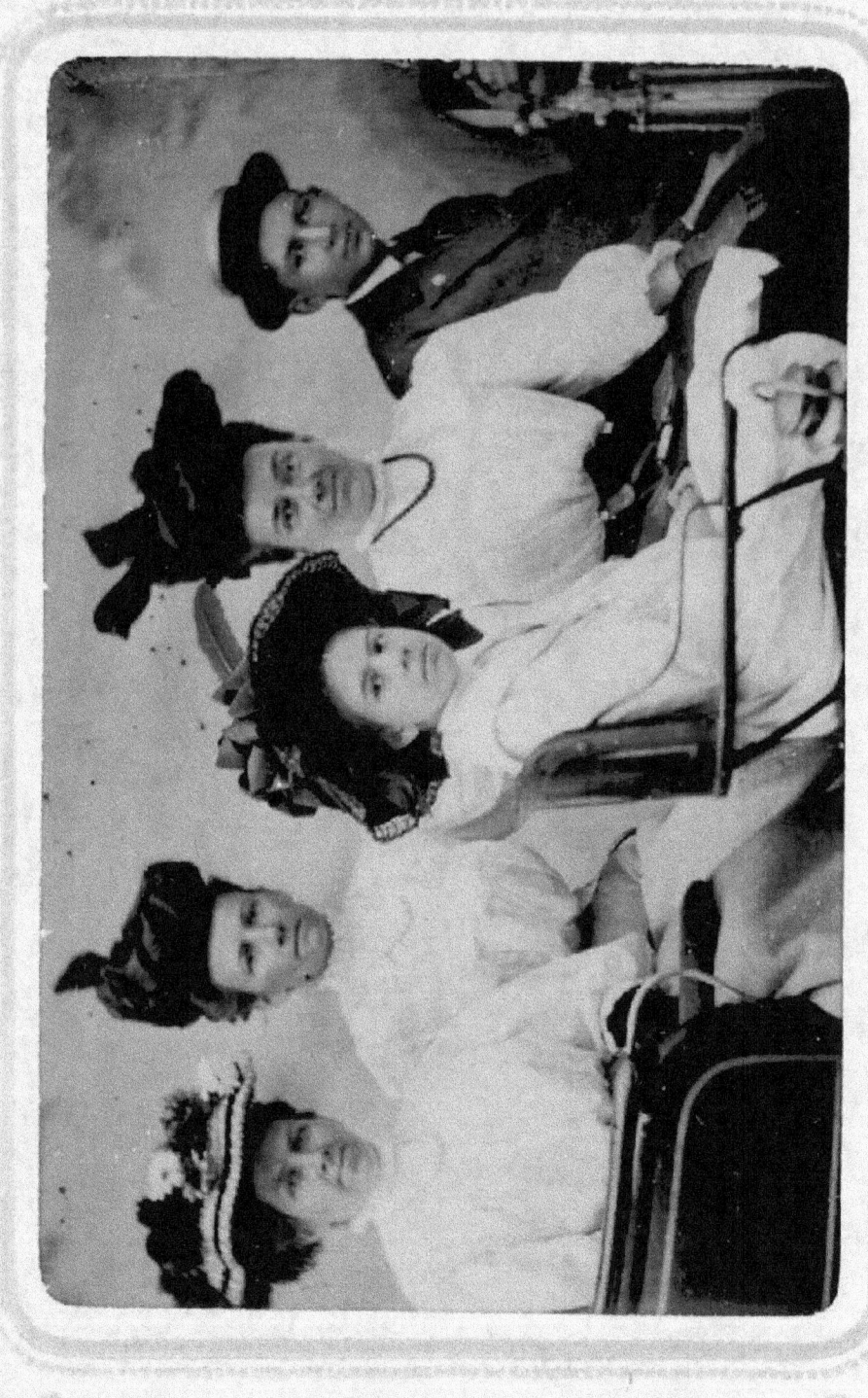

his sister Florence "Flossie" 11 with their mother Luella 30 pose in a car that looks most closely like a Präsident against a landscape backdrop. The car might even be a carriage with a steering handle added.

I discovered another picture on Ebay with the same siblings. Examining the two pictures it appears that they were taken at the same session.

Research on FamilySearch came up with lots of families who had a William and a Florence brother and sister. But I found one where the ages were two years apart. They fit right in the proper time. At least they represent typical immigrants. The family came to America from Canada in 1901. Their father Michael T,

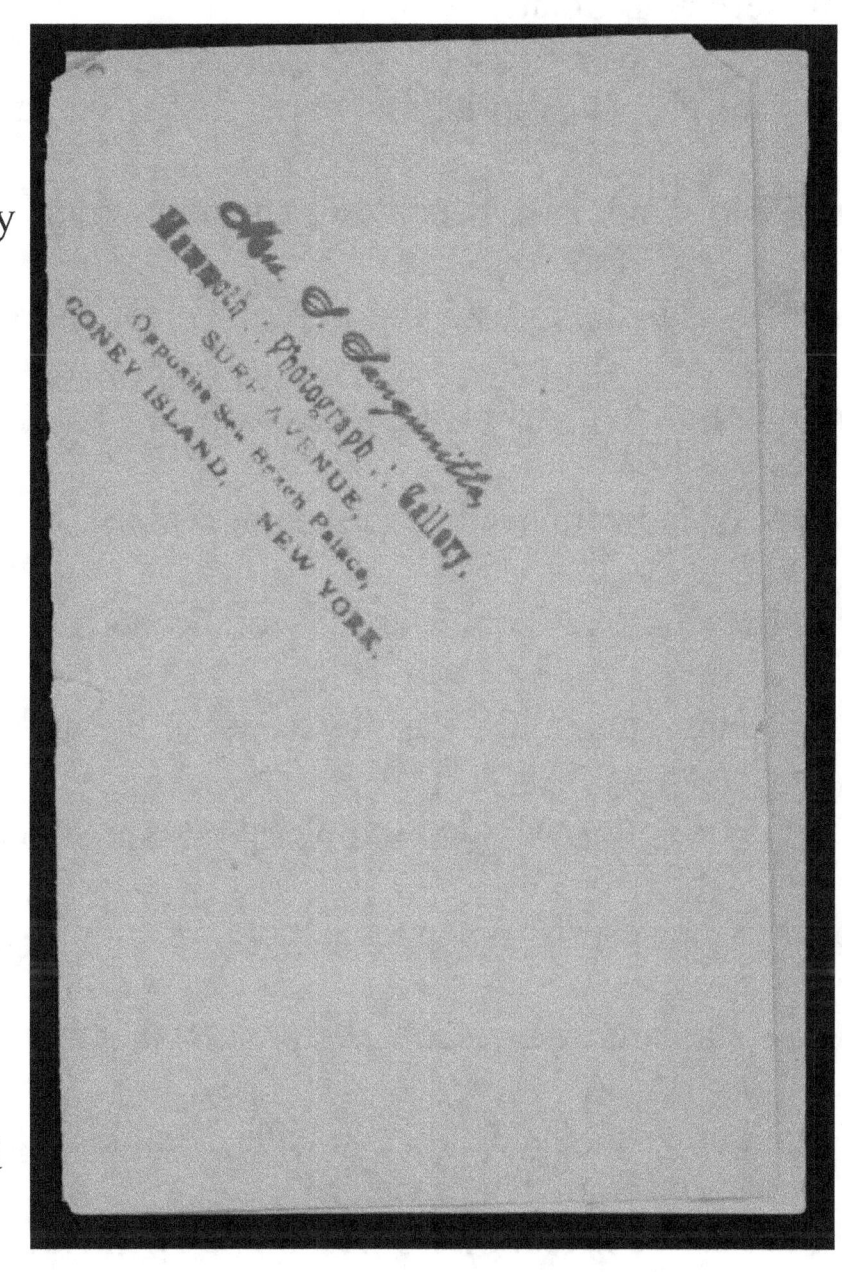

age 32, is a Brew Crewman, at a brewery "Working on own account." The other children are another son, Manford 5, and daughter Fidelis, born four years later in New York. Michael rents their house in Alexandria Bay, Jefferson County.[13]

The elderly proprietress, Sarah Mann Sangunitto might have greeted them and she or an assistant took the photograph. Sarah is married to James J. Sangunitto who was born in Genoa, Italy in 1838. His parents brought him to the United States when he was an infant. He moved to Coney Island with his father when he was 19. He and Sarah have six children: James, Albert, Mabel, Leon, Robert, and Richard.

James Sangunitto was the keeper of the makeshift Norton's Point Light. His duties included setting up two oil lamps on poles every night, to warn the vessels. When the couple was not rescuing survivors from the occasional wreck he and Sarah operated the tintype photography studio located opposite the Sea Beach Palace and railroad depot. Sarah, who purchased the invention from Adolphe-Alexandre Martin of France is credited for having the first tintype studio in Coney Island.

After a permanent lighthouse was constructed in 1890, James continued employment as a watchman.[14]

A 1911 edition of The Brookland Eagle reports that Sarah died on Thursday, January 26, 1911.[15]

James who by then was Coney Island's oldest resident died in 1936.

I don't know if mammoth referred to the size of the studio or if they had bones or a replica of an ancient creature. On a map I see a Mammoth city nearby. They might have had more than one studio space. A client might have chosen a beach scene like the one on the next page or the automobile scene. Maybe the settings changed frequently, one year the beach, the next year the car. It's possible that the Cobey family is in this picture but I can't be sure. Sarah Sangunitto's operation was very popular judging by the number of tintypes that still have the paper mat with the studio stamp which can be found on Pintrest, Instagram, Fickr, and Ebay.

Made by the company Nesselsdorfer Wagenbau-Fabriks-Gesellschaft A.G. the 1897 Präsident is the first car to be manufactured in Austria-Hungary, the creation of Leopold Sviták and Hans Ledwinka. The vehicle made with wooden bodywork that is placed on an iron frame was more of a carriage without horses than a car in the modern sense. It was steered with handlebars; tilting forward and backward changed gears. It seated four and had a vinyl top that only covered the rear seats.

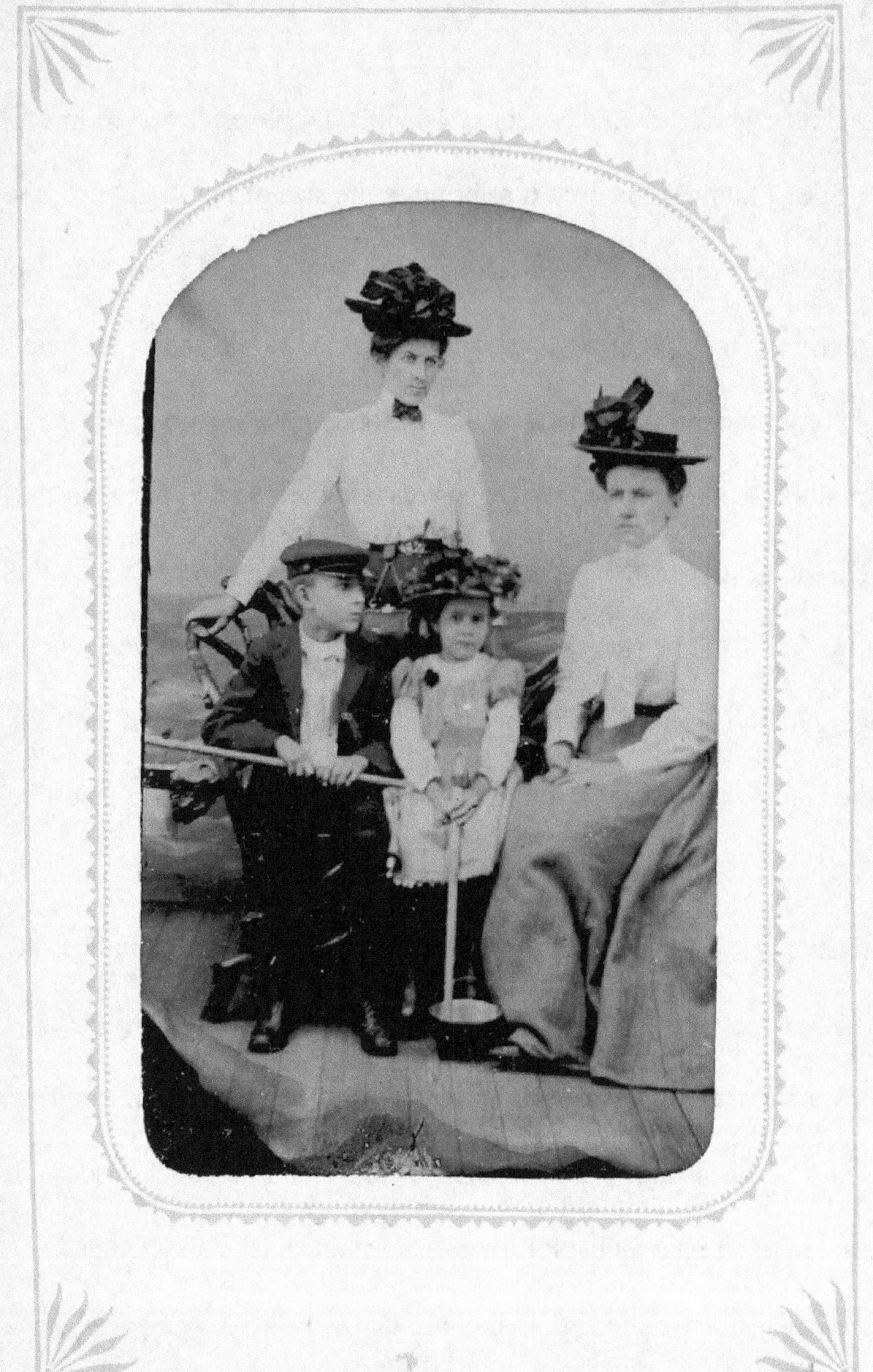

The two axles had a suspension of semi-elliptical leaf springs. The wheels were similar to that of a horse carriage, but with rubber tires. This automobile had a two-cylinder four-stroke spark-ignition Benz engine placed next to the rear axle. It had a two-speed transmission. It could reach a speed of nineteen miles per hour.[16]

Here is a charming scene that might be the same studio with the father wearing a chauffeur cap prop with two daughters posing in an identical car and backdrop, perhaps minutes after Willy and Flossie.

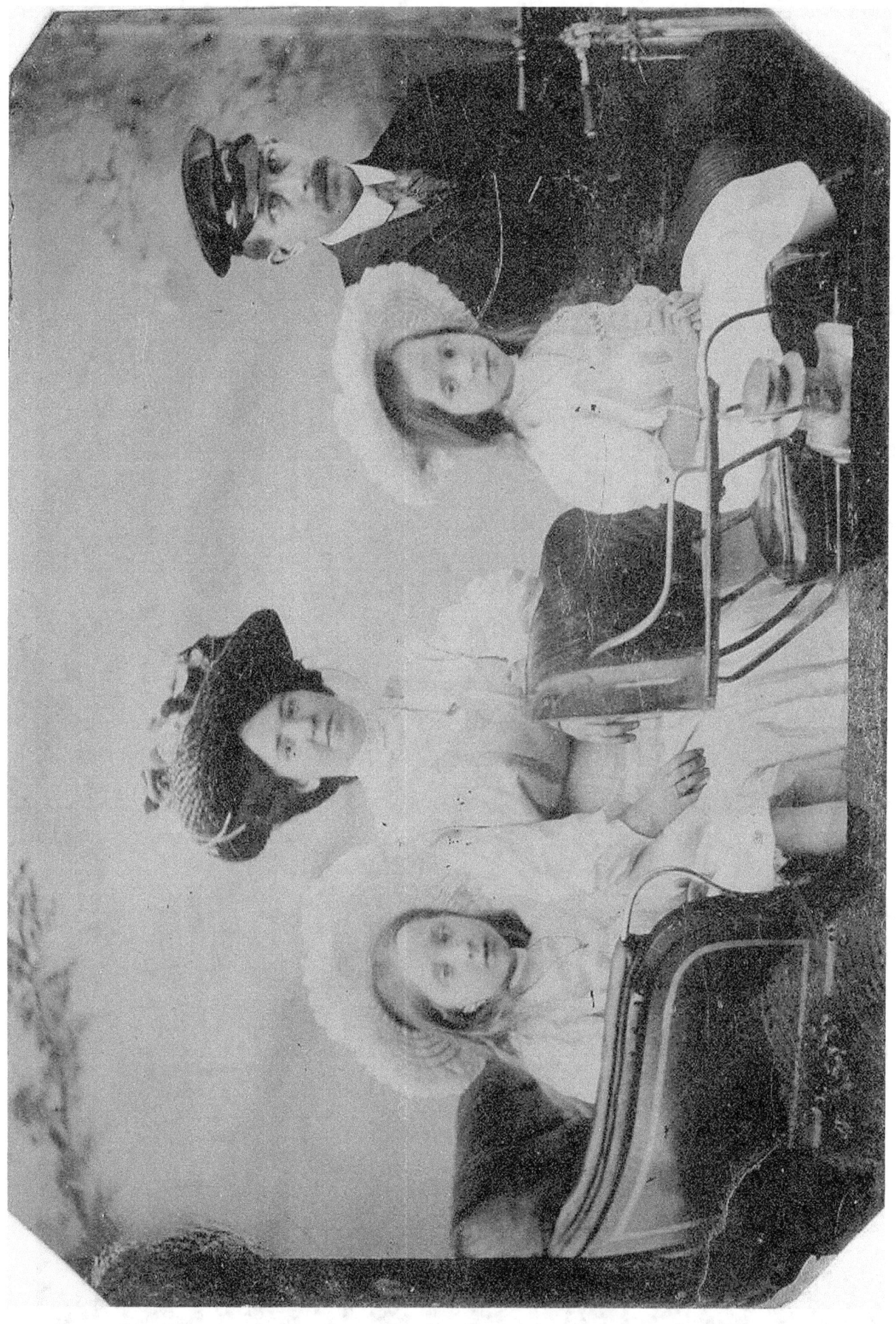

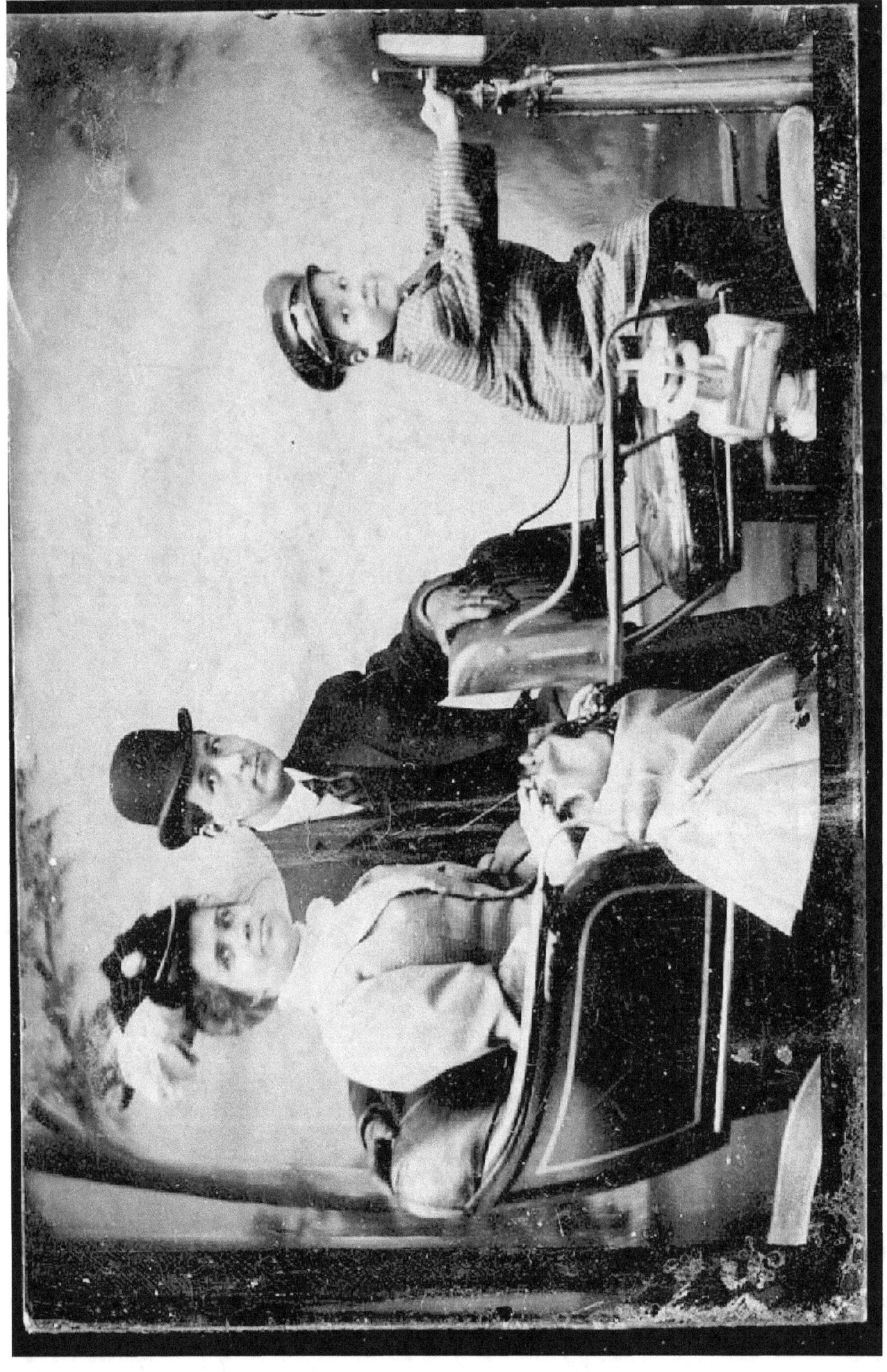

Here we have a "candid" of a family in a car might have also have been taken at Mammoth Photograph Gallery. For a few minutes the boy, wearing a chauffeur cap prop, is the boss, driving his amused beautiful mother, and his father who according to social morays must hide his emotions.

On the next page we have a picture from the same studio showing another customer who chose to wear a chaufer hat. I wonder if they got to keep it.

These were on auction on Ebay at the same time. Either the studio was very prolific or the same type of car and same backdrop were a popular combination.

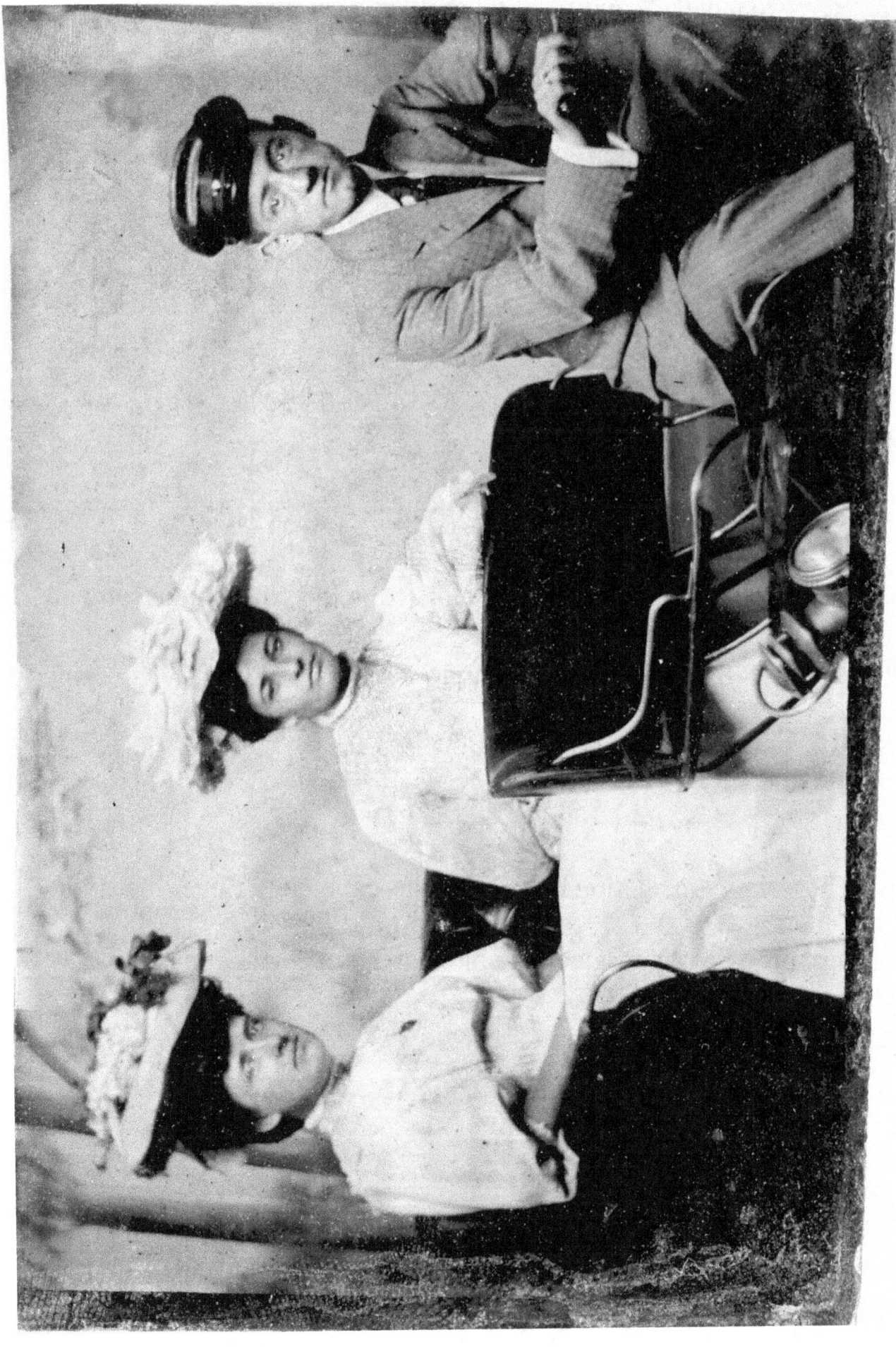

Here we have another darling picture of a father with his daughter.

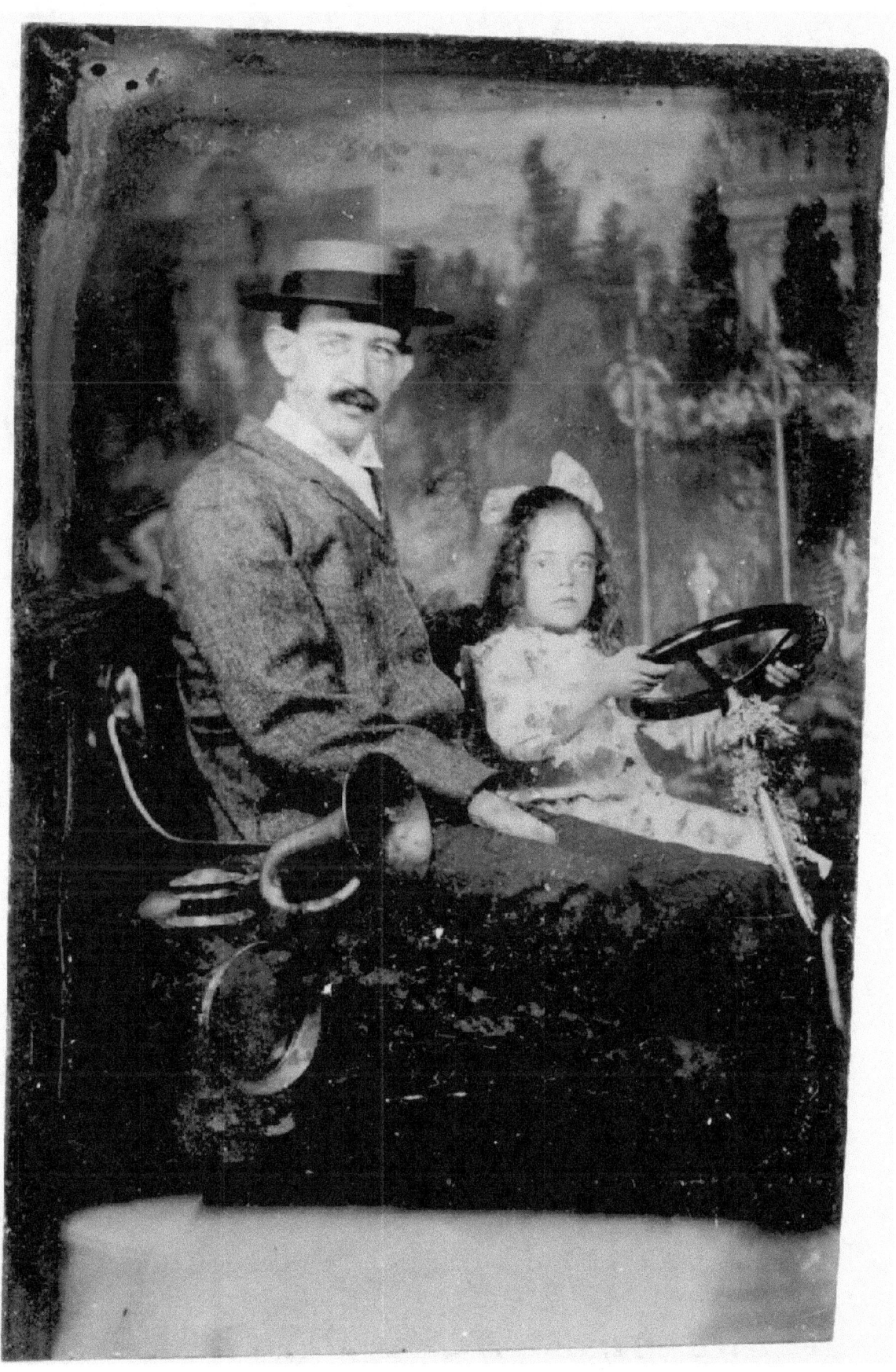

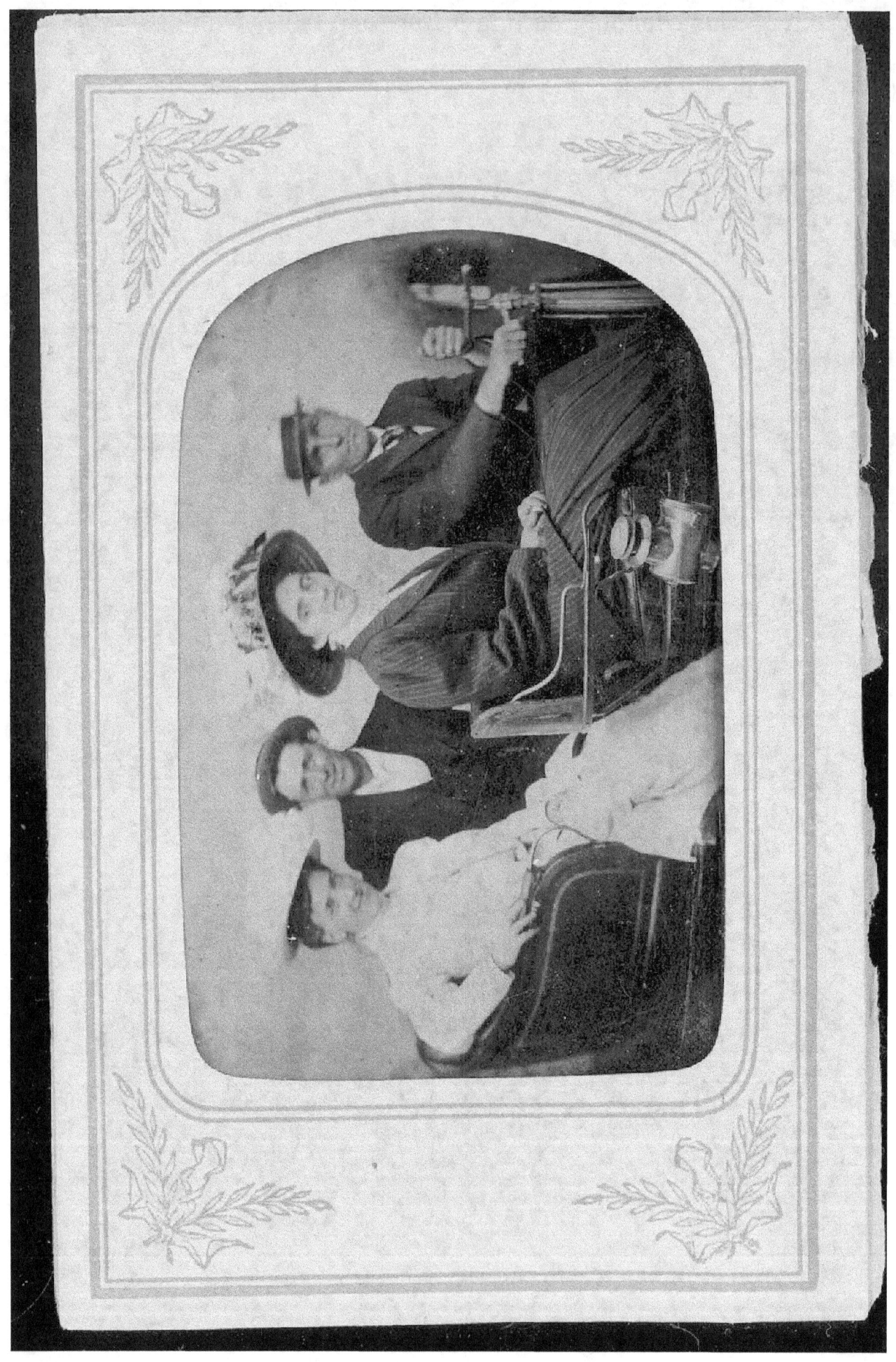

On previous page another tintype

which might be a

Sangunitto tintype without the

chauffeur hat.

                      And on the next page we have

a similar car and pose a group

which is an example of the

photographer being out of

horizontal mats or too cheap to buy

vertical ones.

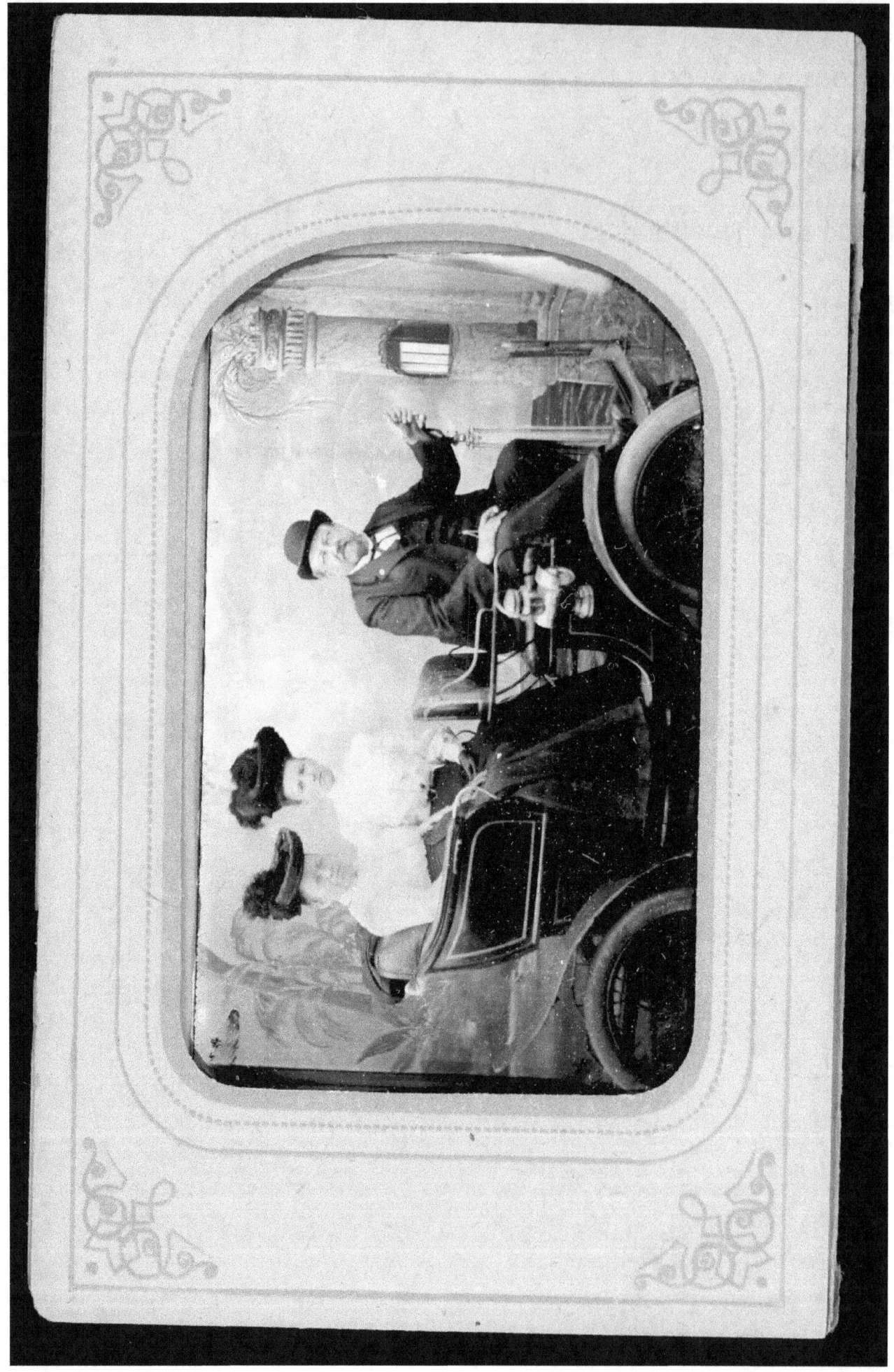

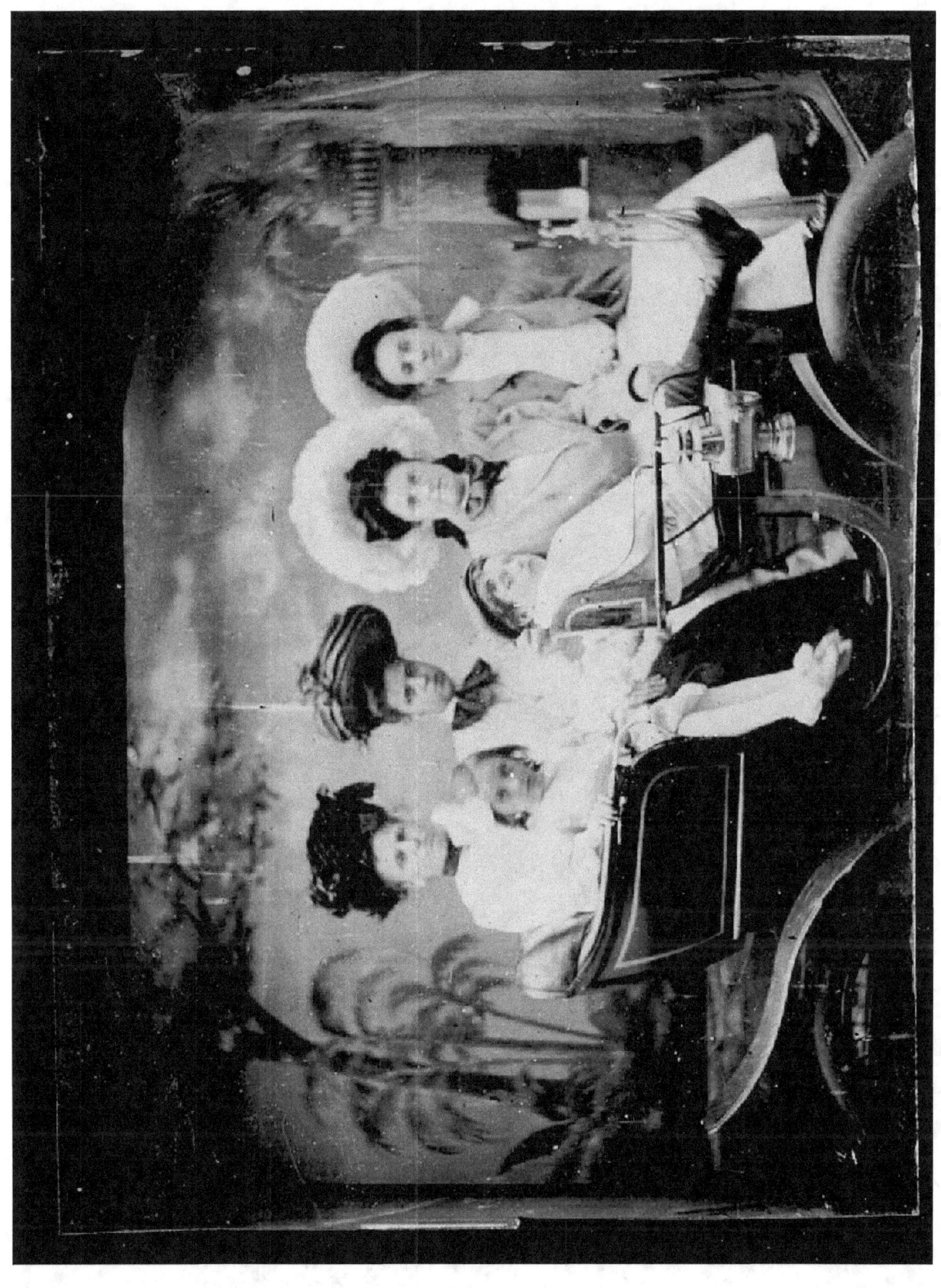

One with the same type of car with a different back drop.

Pretty Lady. Car closely matches 1902 Cadillac Tonneau Cadillac Motors Co., Detroit, MI. Backdrop looks like a road.

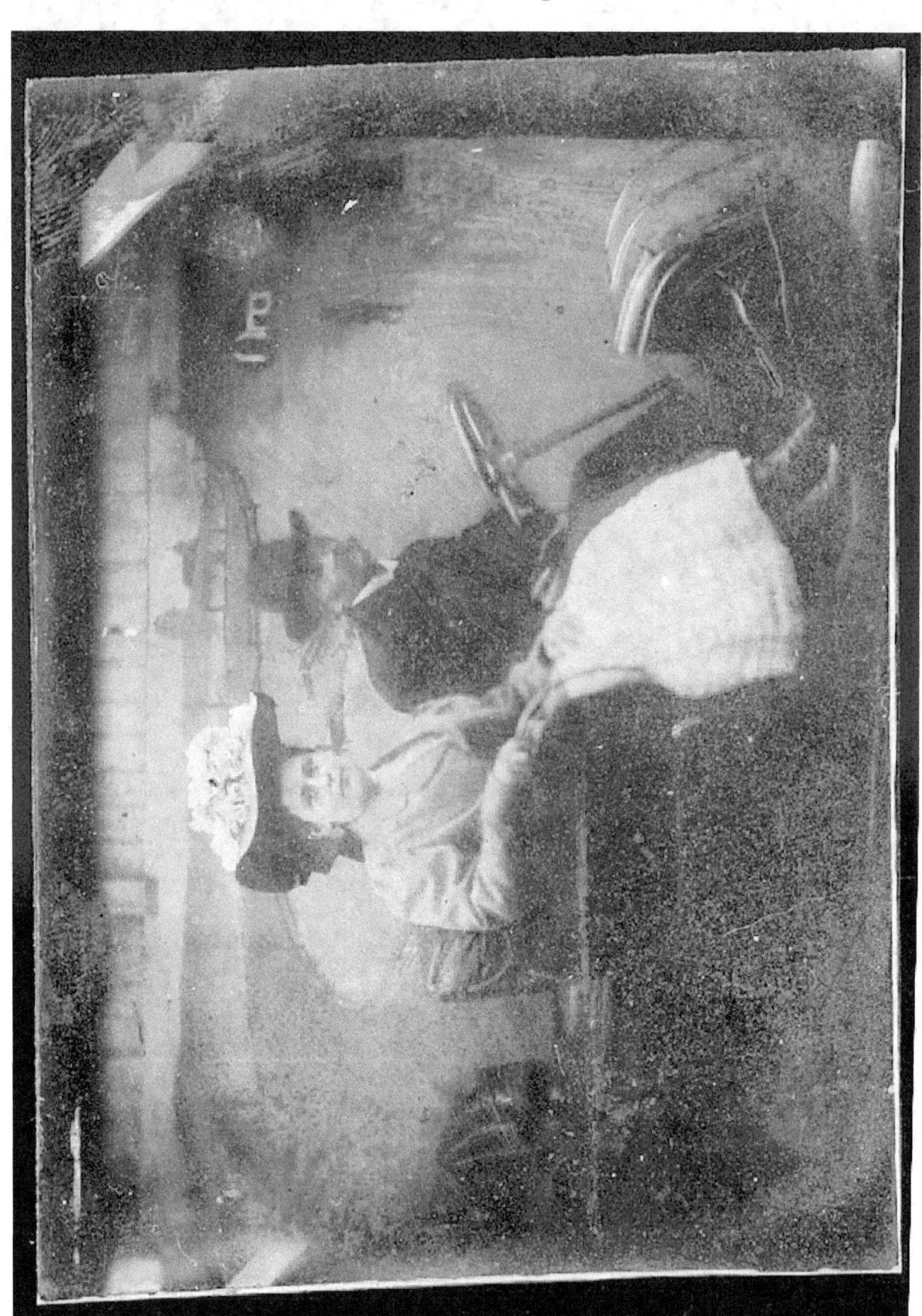

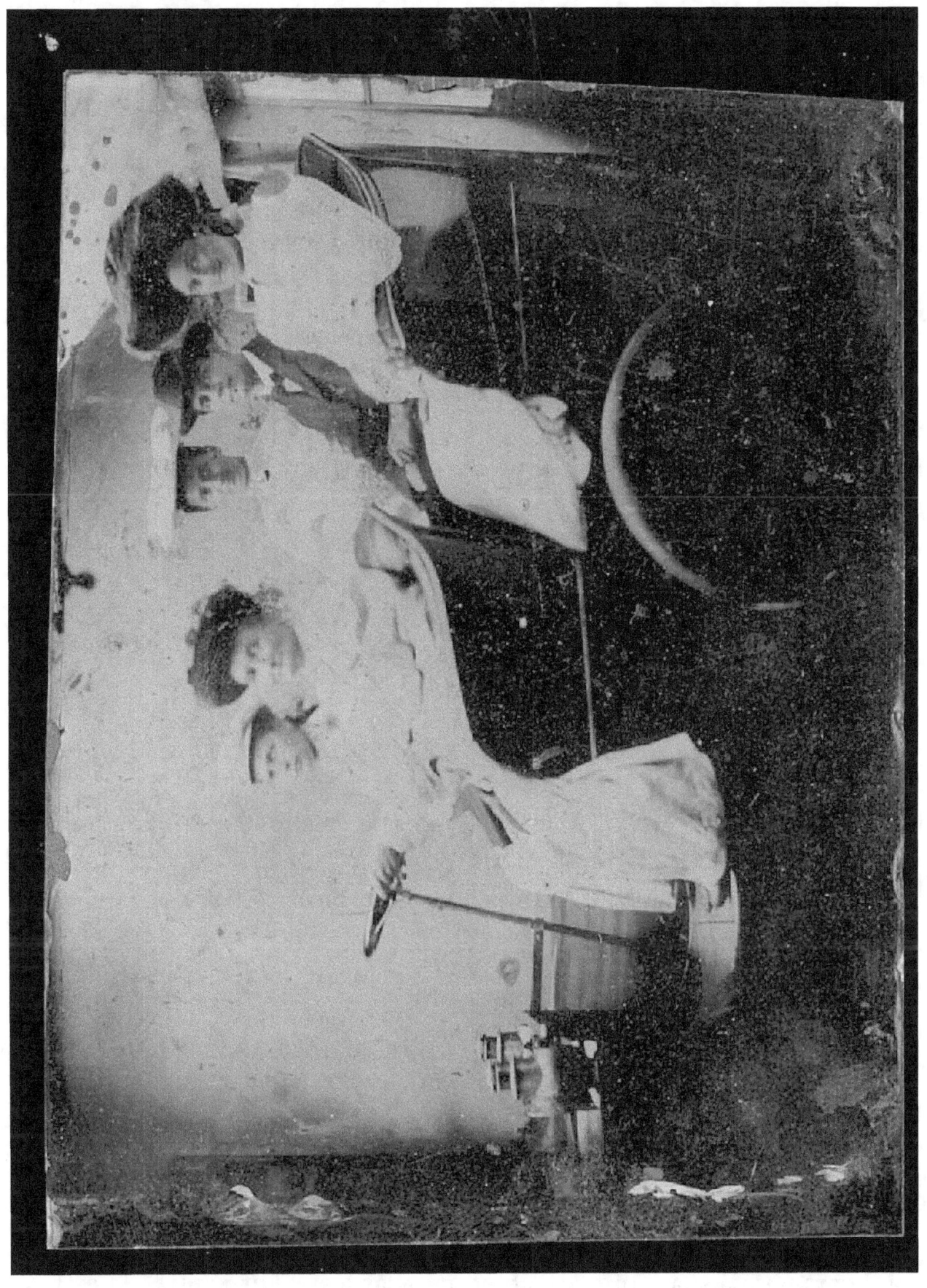

In another scene from an amusement park or carnival, we have a group that includes ladies wearing hats posing in a car that might be a

35

1903 Cadillac with an added rear entrance tonneau, an open rear passenger compartment, rounded like a barrel. The car is powered by a reliable and sturdy ten-horsepower single-cylinder engine. The two-seater runabout cost $750; adding the optional detachable tonneau added $100 to the price. The entire body was bolted to the chassis and could be lifted without removing or disconnecting any plumbing or wiring. "The front of the car had a sloping, curved, false hood and radiator. The car was advertised as having six and a half horsepower. The twenty-two-inch wood wheels had twelve spokes."[17]

A similar group (next picture) looks like they are posing in a poorly made studio prop of a 1902 Rambler Model C, a single cylinder engine car made by Thomas B. Jeffery of Chicago, Illinois. Jeffery began commercial production at his Kenosha, Wisconsin factories in 1902 and by the end of the year had produced 1,500 motorcars, one-sixth of all existing in the USA at the time. The first production Ramblers were tiller-steered. Rambler innovated various design features and was the first to equip cars with a spare tire.[18] To buy one was a steal at $750.[19] The model in the photograph looks astonishingly like the prototype.

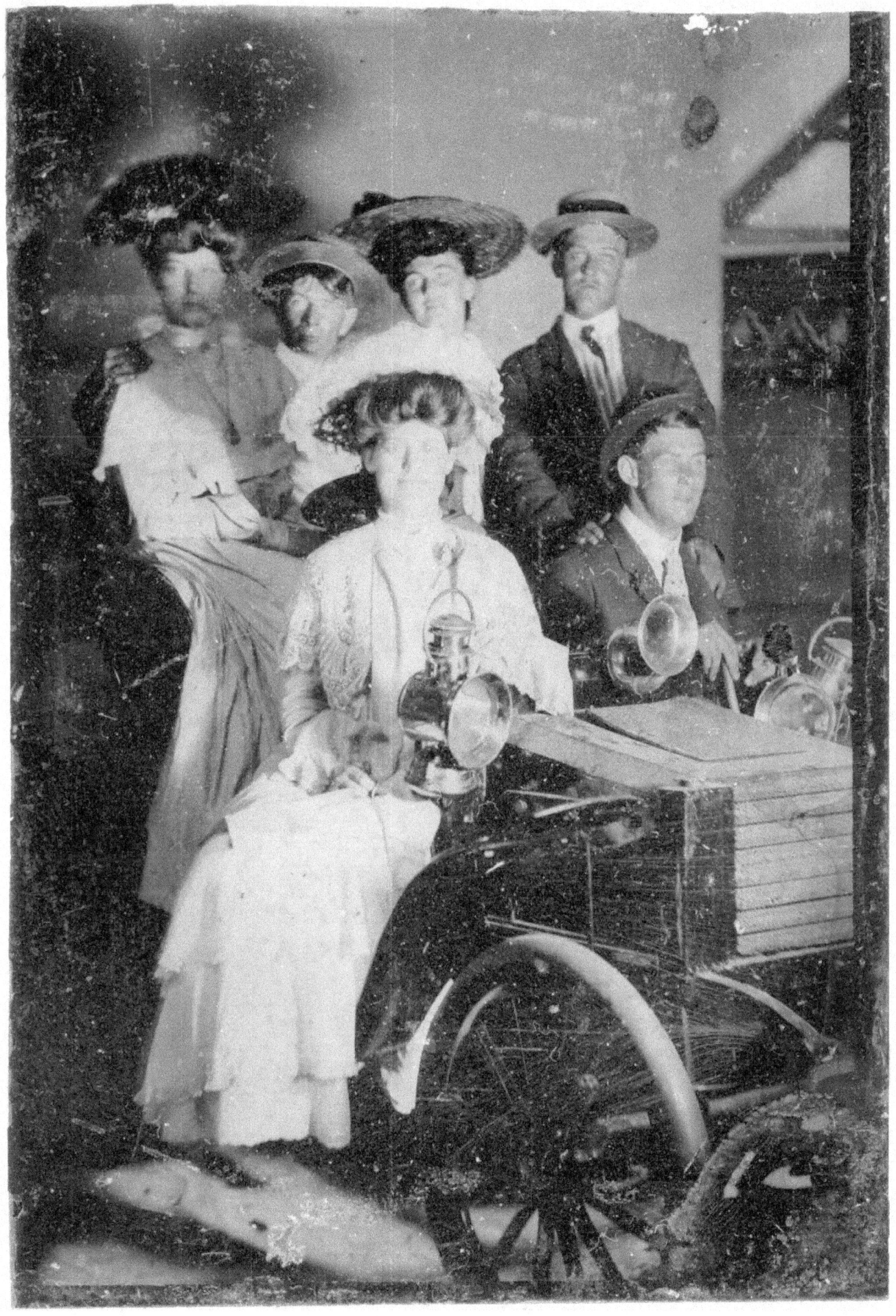

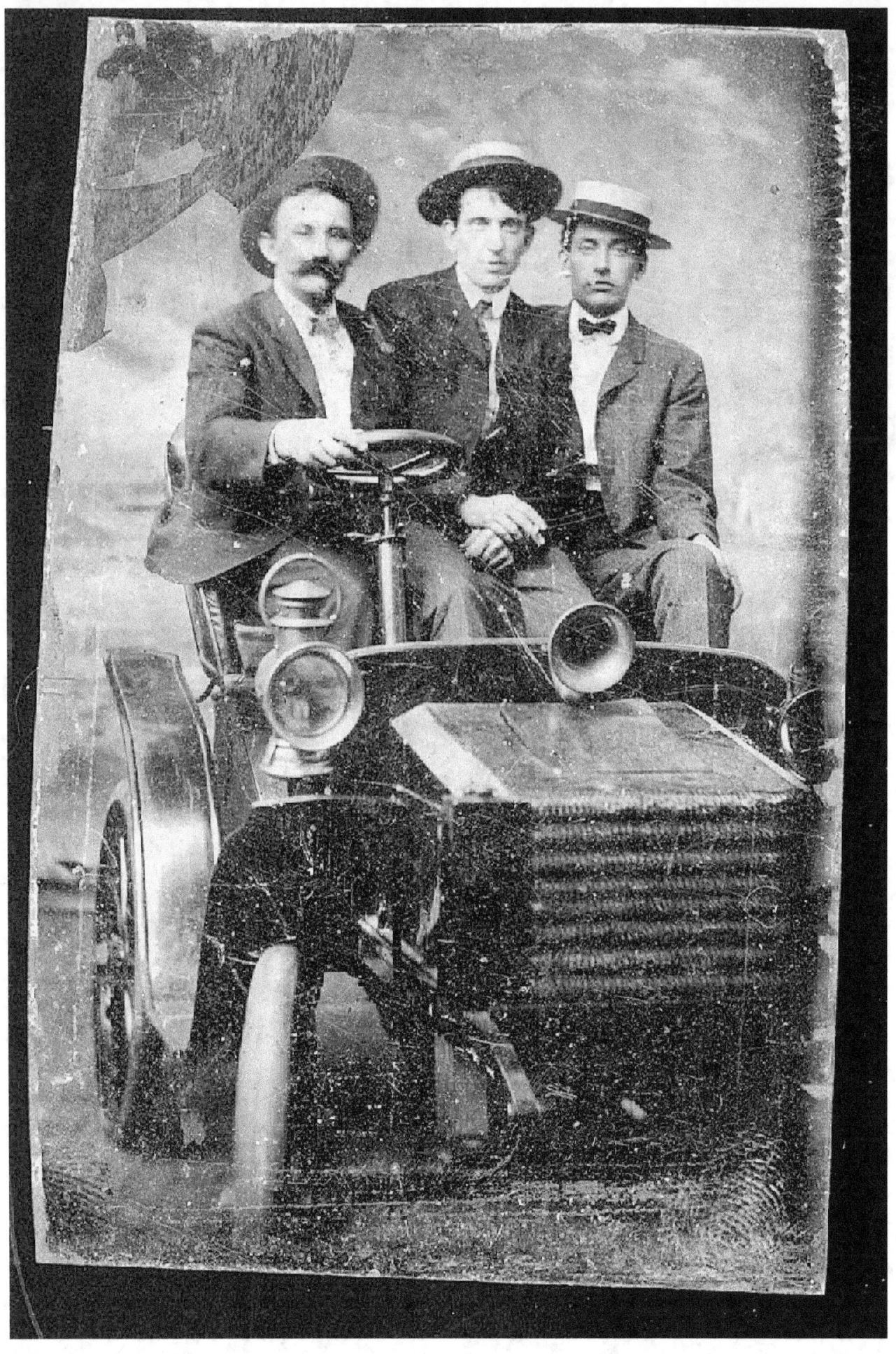

Previous page. Here we have three men posed in What might be a 1908 Cadillac Runabout..

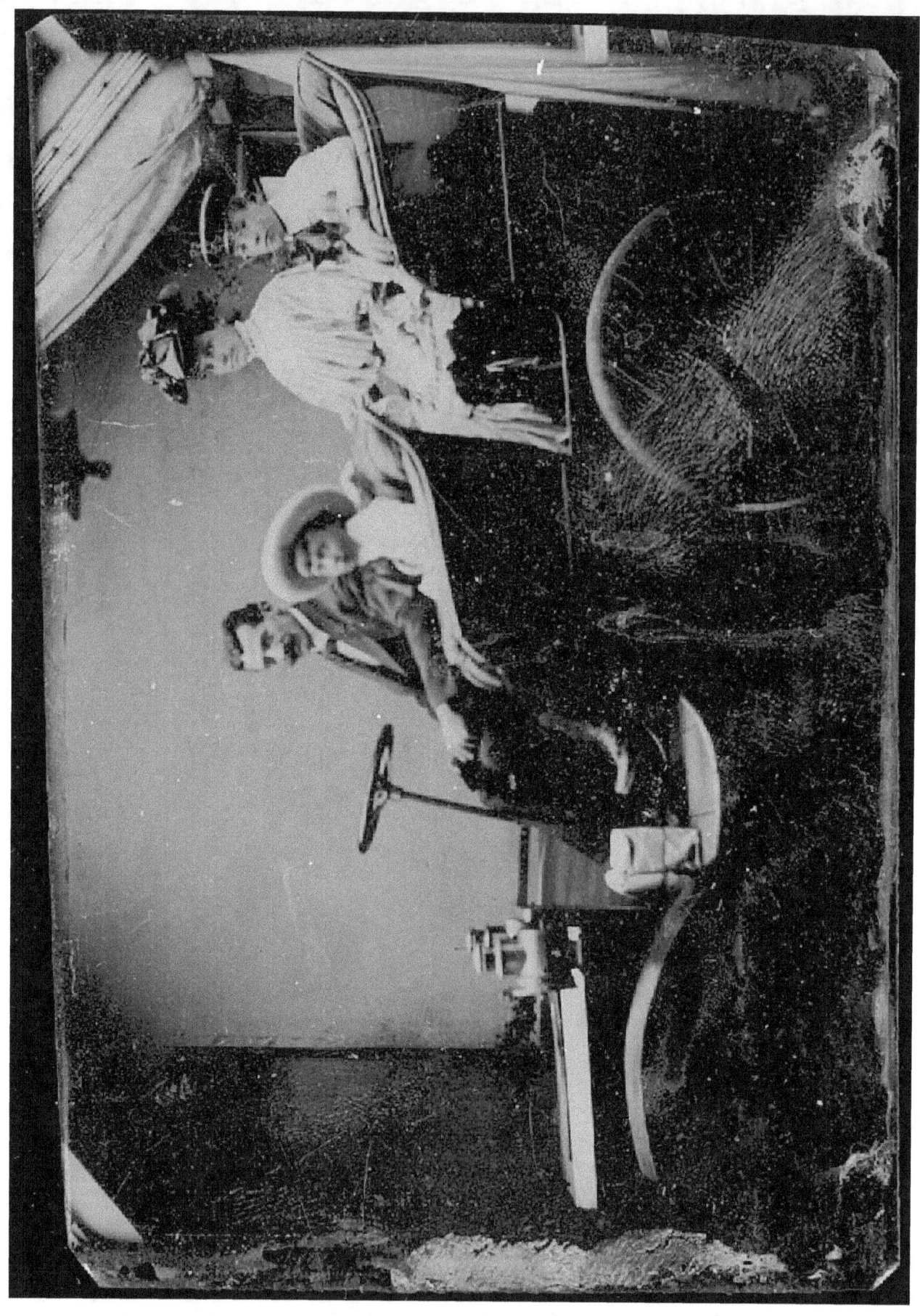
Another family posing in a prop car.

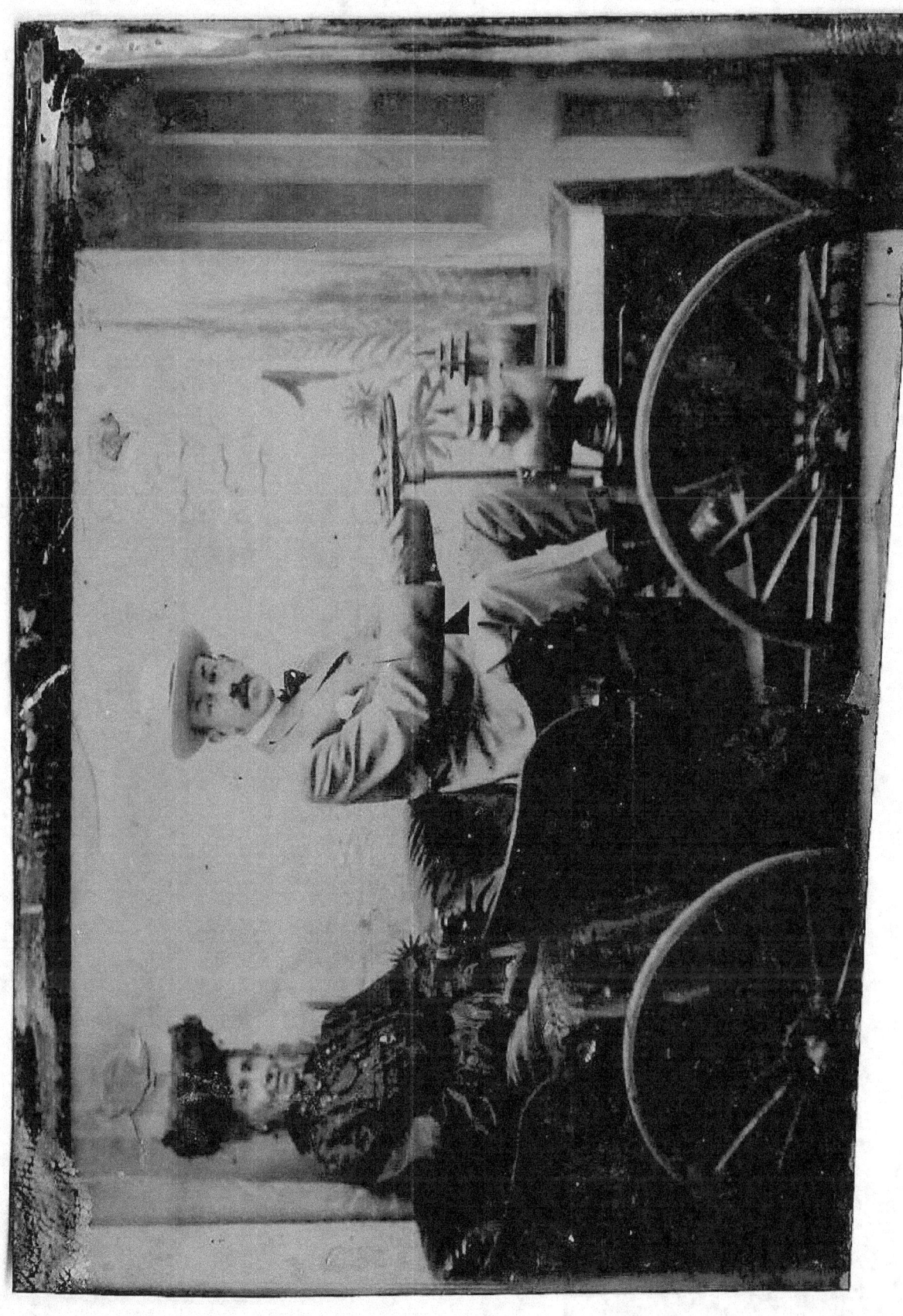

The tintypist who photographed this couple in an unidentified car depended on the mat to hide the edges of the backdrop.

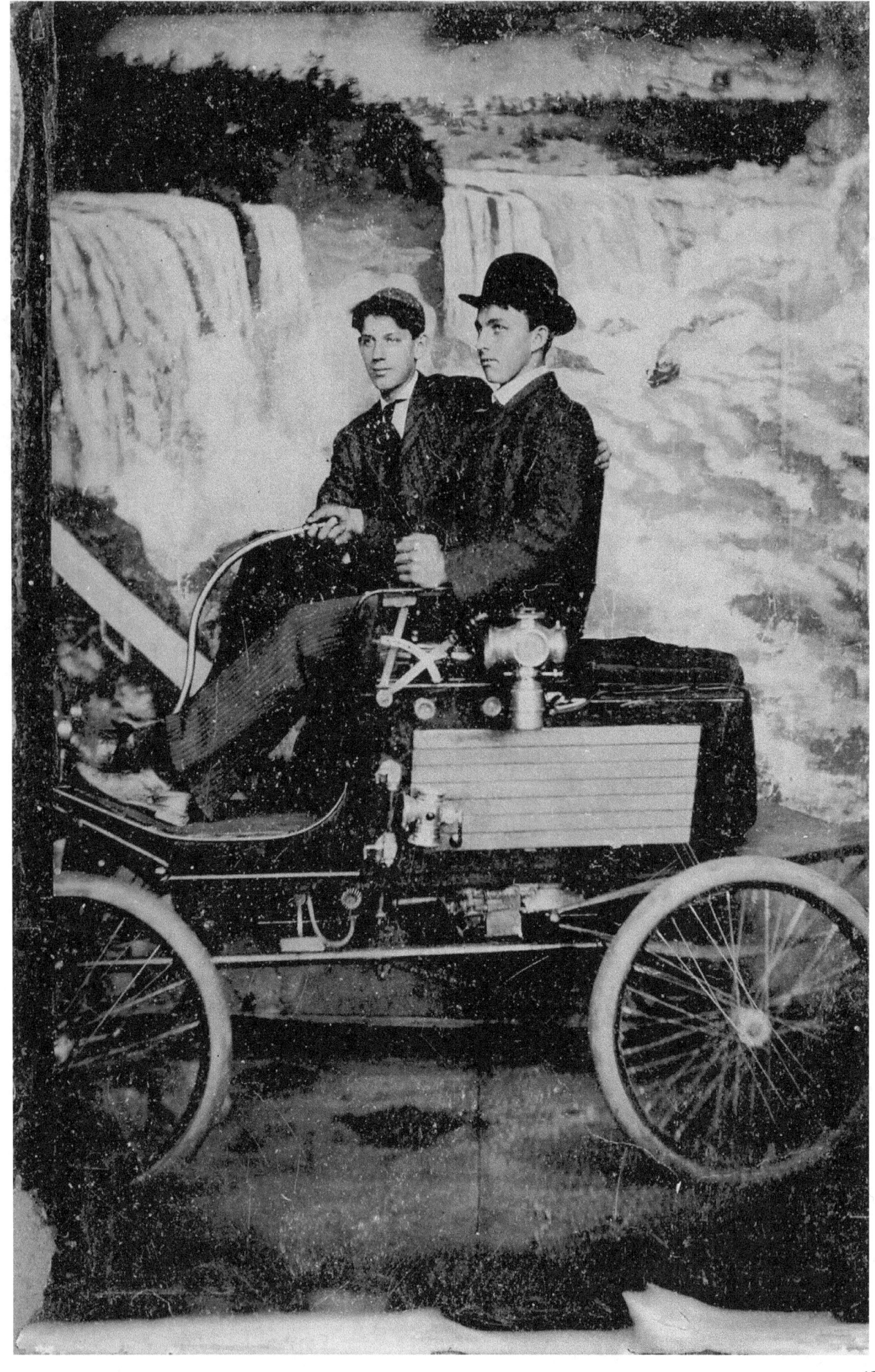

Now we arrive in Rochester New York where J. R. Martin and Edward Wagoner (previous page) who might reside at the address written on the paper frame, 95 North Street, pose in front of a Niagara Falls backdrop in what looks like a Milwaukee Automobile Company 1900 steam-powered Mobile Runabout[20]

Obviously, these two transients didn't have the money to buy a $750.[21] car, but they could get their picture taken in it.

I could find no information on Martin. I found a Fred Edward Wagoner on Family Search who was born on 18 October 1886 which puts him in the right time to be a teen in the photograph. He died on 20

July 1961 and is buried at Woodlawn Cemetery in Canandaigua, Ontario, New York. There is a military service date of 10 September 1919 but the significance of the date is not stated, probably a discharge.[22] Which means that he served in Company A. 108 Infantry during WWI.[23]

The Rochester directory lists an Edward Wagoner in 1906 – 1908, with the profession of coremaker (a person who makes sand cores for metal castings or clay cores for iron pipe or metal cores for building tile[24]) who had a different address each year.[25] This is exactly as they are written:1906 rear 330 Lyell avenue h 1501 brown, 1907 falls h 74 smith, 1908 h 402 St. paul.

I looked up the 95 North Street address to see if I could get any information. It might have been a residential area at the time but it is a business area now though it

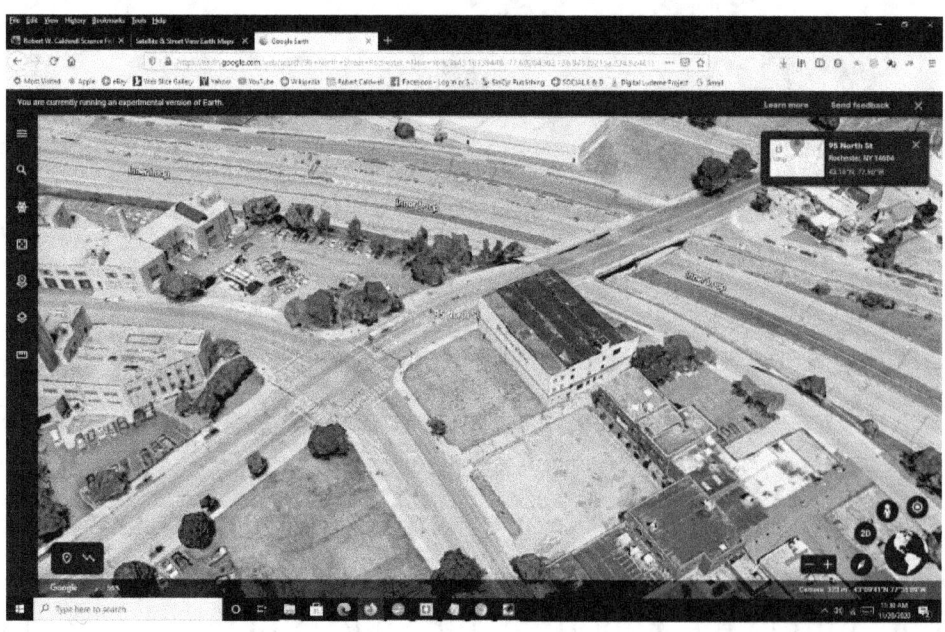

Just for fun I checked to see where the site was in relation to the George Eastman Museum.

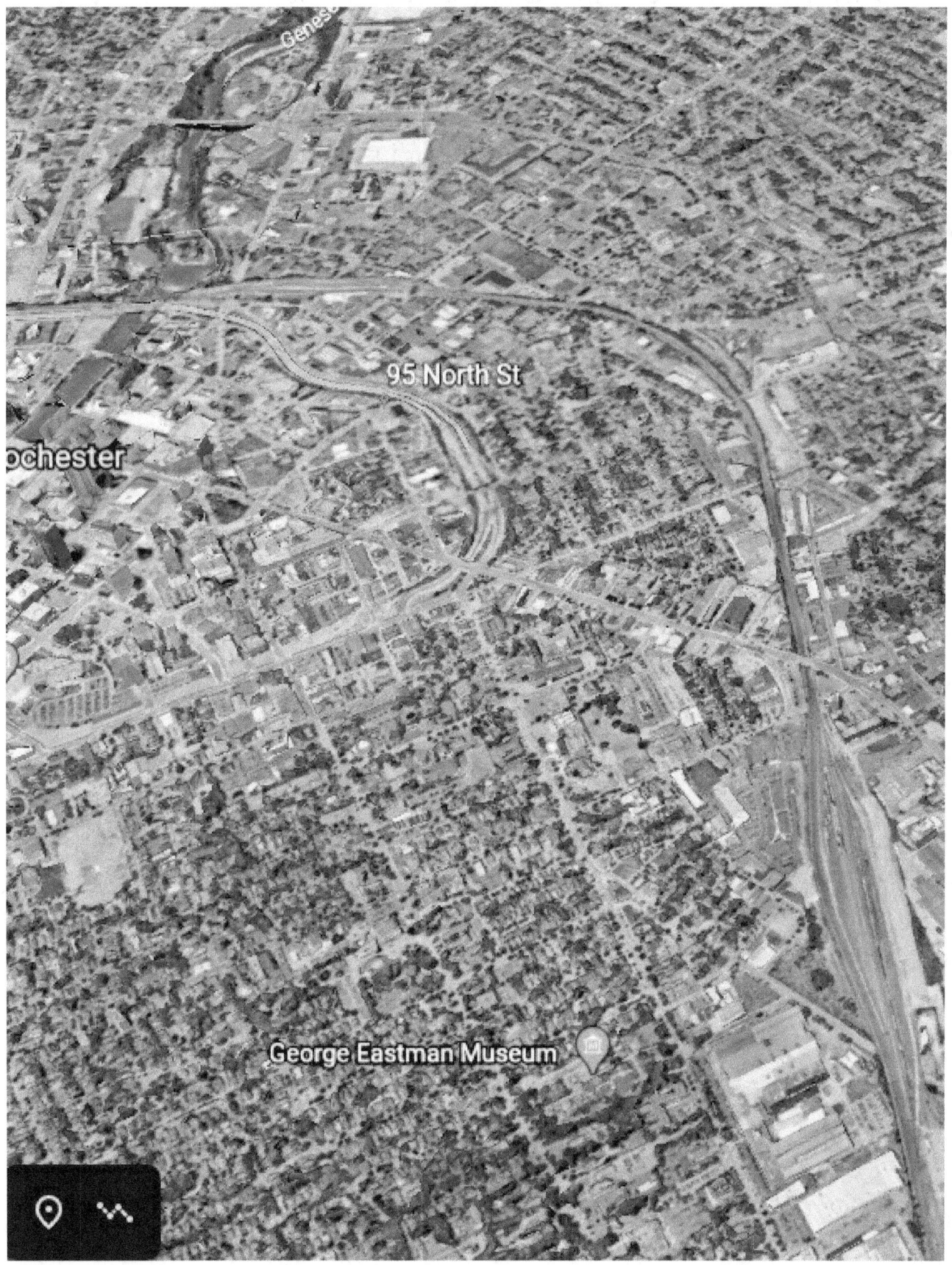

has obviously seen better days and appears to be unoccupied.

The Milwaukee steam car, made by the Milwaukee Automobile Company in Milwaukee, Wisconsin, used a five-horsepower vertical two-cylinder engine, with a single chain drive. The company offered various body styles in addition to the runabout, a four-passenger surrey,[26] probably the Model E which had a canvas top, the Model C, which also had an optional top and looks like the one in the picture except some pictures show a car with the steering L shaped tiller on the right side, the Model H, a four-seater which had a rearward-facing seat, and Models M and O which were boxy delivery vehicles.

The car in the photograph is most likely similar to this description of what was probably the prototype. It was said to have a complete steam plant automatic in action that is carried within the carriage body. The wheels were twenty-eight inches with metal spokes and two and one half inch pneumatic tires with a tread of four feet. It had two-inch axles that were four feet ten inches apart. The total weight with tanks and a full boiler was 700 pounds. It carried forty miles of supplies. The operator sat on the right-side steering with left foot, and controlled the steam valve and brake with his left hand and foot. (The car in the photograph has the tiller in the middle) The water glass and steam gauge were "located convenient for inspection."

An advertisement says it has a seamless boiler and tanks. Another advertisement said that they are making deliveries. Another ad reads they "Can Supply Complete Tubular Gears with Hubs, Axles, Compensation Device, Steering Rig, etc." Another says it has seamless steel air and gasoline tanks. Interestingly, gasoline was used to heat the water.[27]

We leave Rochester and take a long detour to the West Coast where we meet this nicely dressed couple posed in a fanciful touring car against a painted backdrop depicting a hillside with a road as if the car was about to ascend to the Cliff House, a hotel in San Francisco. I saw this on EBay and recognized the building from a family tintype I already had in my collection.

The Cliff House is perched on the headland above the cliffs just north of Ocean Beach, in the Outer Richmond neighborhood.

The building overlooks the site of the Sutro Baths ruins, Seal Rocks, and is part of the Golden Gate National Recreation Area, operated by the National Park Service (NPS).

The first Cliff House was built in 1863 to serve the throngs of San

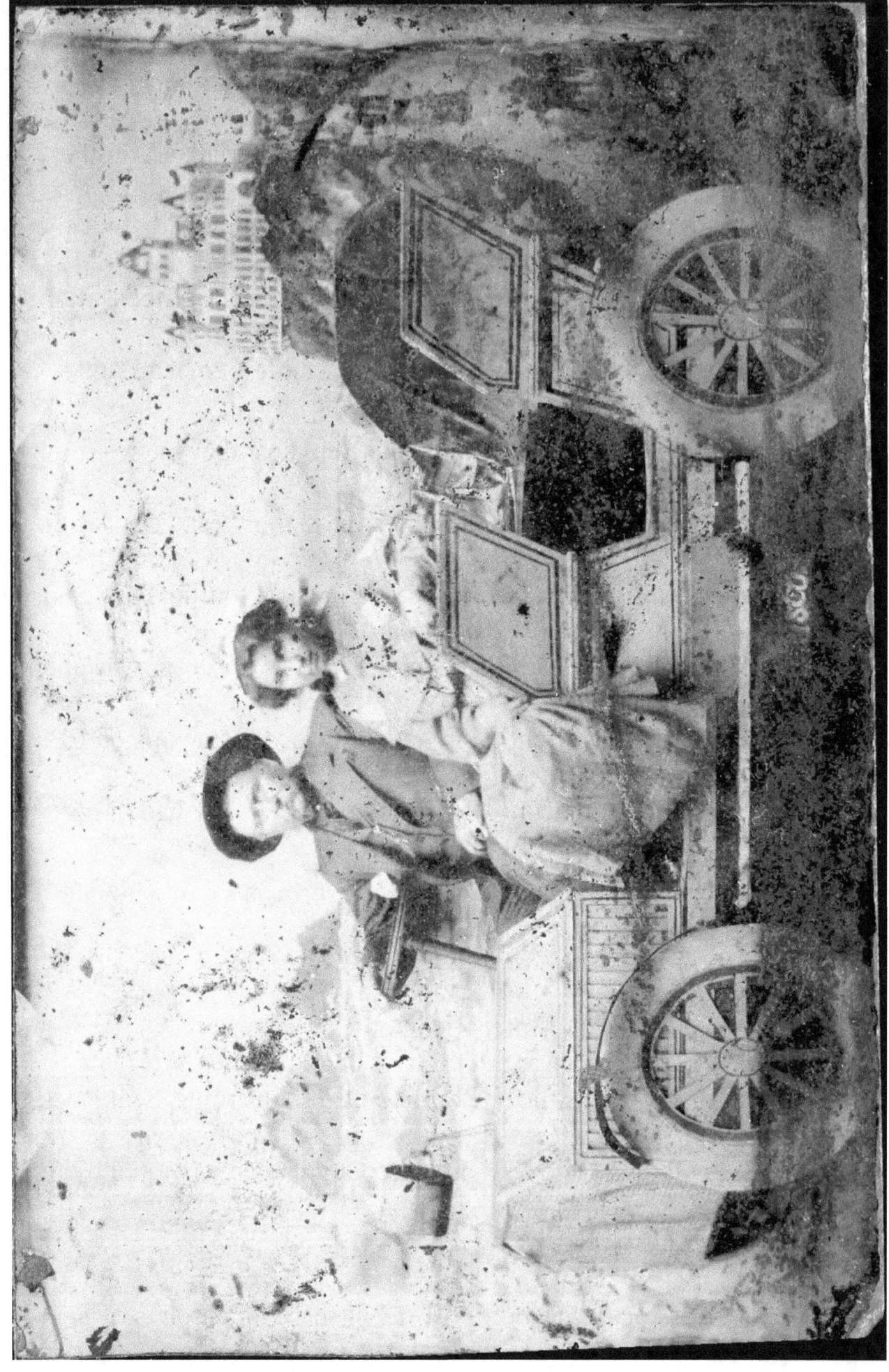

Franciscan pleasure-seekers who traveled to the area on steam trains, bicycles, carts, and horse wagons on Sunday excursions. Later a horse race track was built nearby.

The growth of nearby Golden Gate Park attracted beach travelers, and people coming to watch sea lions sunning themselves on Seal Rocks just off the cliffs.

The structure in this backdrop is the second Cliff House built in c.1900. It was a seven-story Victorian Chateau, called by some "the Gingerbread Palace." Sutro Baths also opened that year in a small cove nearby. The baths included six large indoor swimming pools, a museum, a skating rink, and other fun things. The pleasure seekers could view a collection of stuffed animals, artwork, and historic items at both the Cliff House and Sutro Baths.

These tintypes must have been made at a studio in the park or the hotel itself.

The 1896 Cliff House survived the 1906 earthquake with little damage but burned to the ground on the evening of September 7, 1907.[28]

This tintype of three women looks like it was made after the more mundane present structure was built, a far less interesting building that

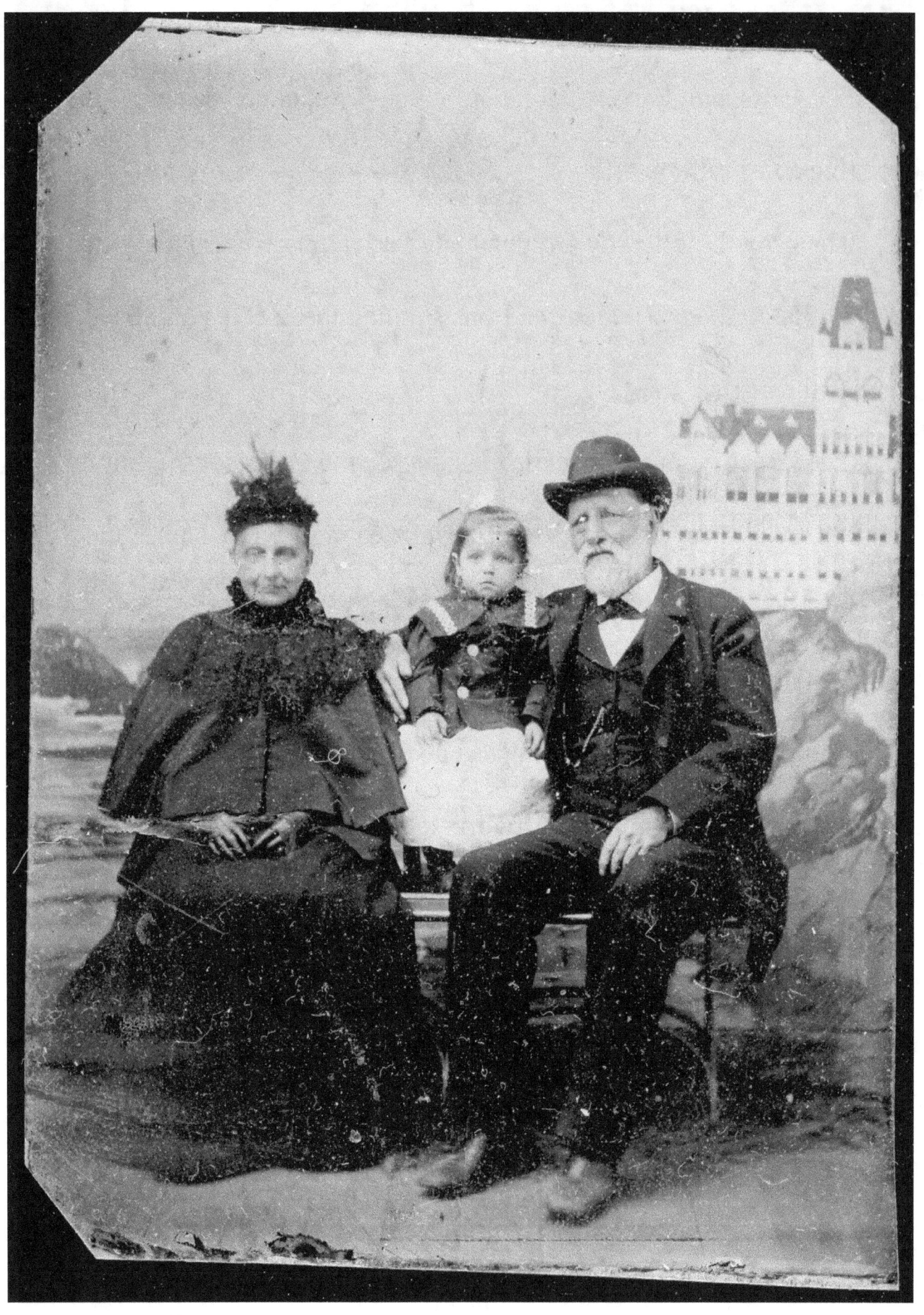

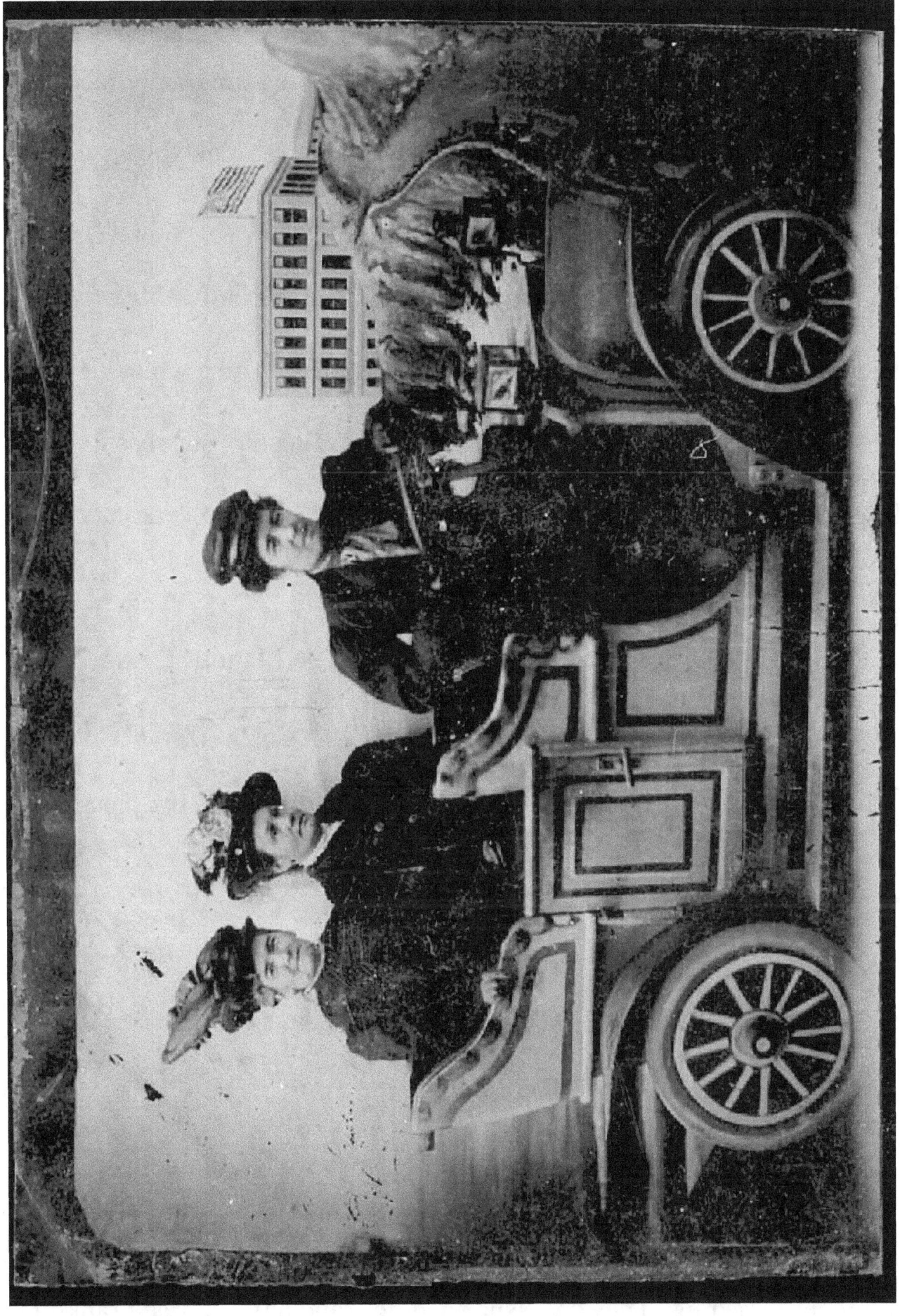

looks like a box with a huge American flag.

The woman on the far left has a pleasant expression on her face.

The next stop is where two women pose in what looks like a Franklin Model A Roadster. They wear fancy hats but the male ties are interesting. The masculine look came into play in the early 1900s as ladies went to work they tended to wear a dark skirt and a white blouse and a ribbon, bow tie, long tie, or something to finish off the basic blouse neckline. They did not fluff it up with lace for the workplace. I can't figure out what is going on with the background.

The Model A was made by the H.H. Franklin Manufacturing Company which was in operation from 1902 to 1934 in Syracuse, New York. The founder, Herbert H. Franklin, not only began in the metal die-casting business – he in fact invented the term 'die cast'.

He entered the automobile business with partner John Wilkinson who was an engineering guru. Franklin cars used air-cooling, which was simpler and more reliable than water cooling.

"The early Franklins were given high-revving, 4-cylinder engines mounted transversely in a lightweight chassis with tubular axles and wooden frame rails. They were sporty, quick, and agile. These Franklin

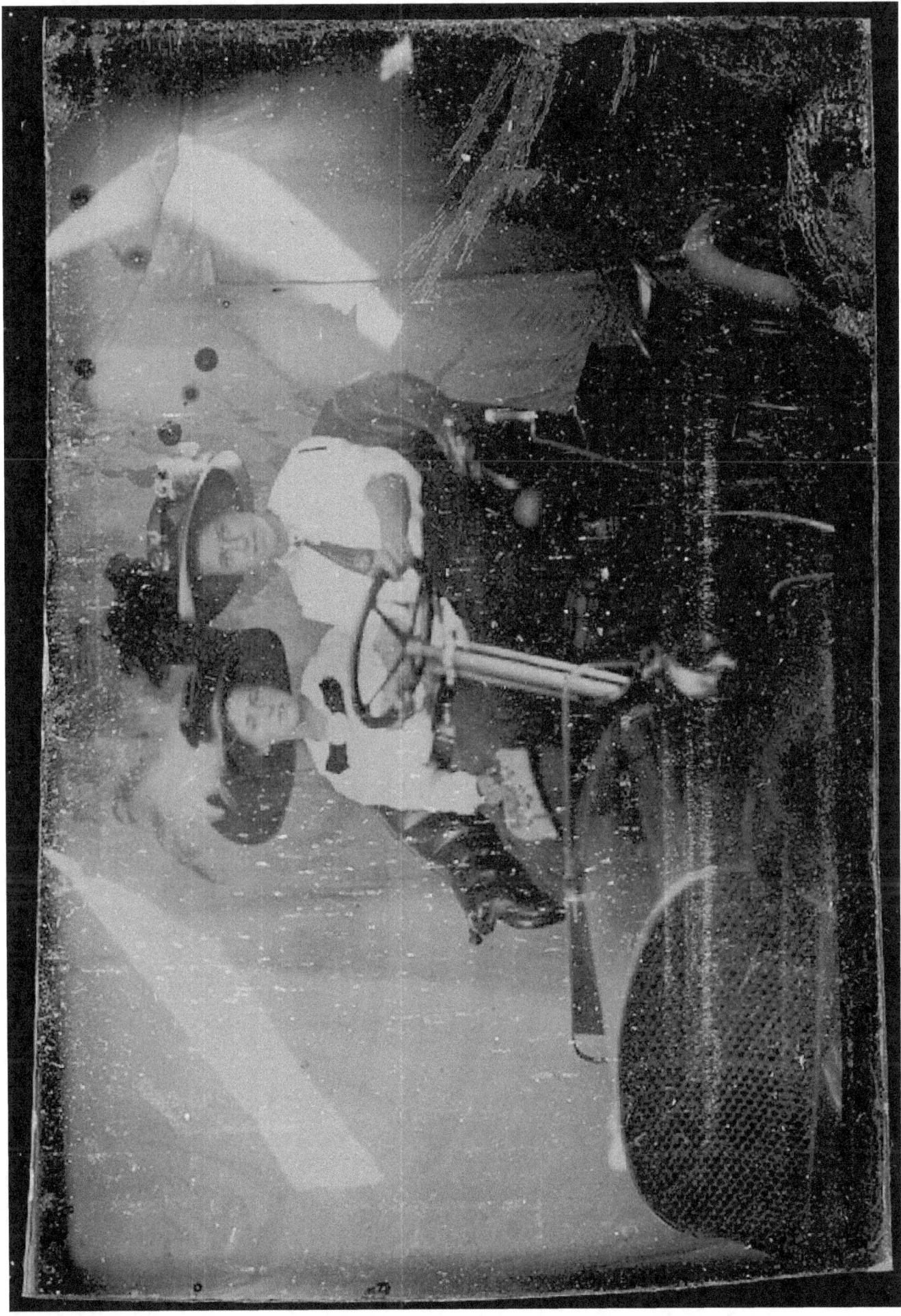

'Cross-Engine' models carried distinct advantages in performance and efficiency over the large bore one and two-cylinder cars in similar size and price class." By 1905, the crankcases had been changed to aluminum, as were the body panels. The drive came from a two-speed transmission through a chain to the rear wheels.

Franklins were Rugged and reliable. These cars set a high standard for the day. The Type A was also available with a rear-entrance tonneau add on which cost an additional $150. This converted the vehicle to a four or five-passenger touring car.

They were powered by a 107.8 cubic-inch four-cylinder engine which had 12 horsepower. The wheelbase measured 80 inches and weighed 1,175 lbs. The total production for that year was around 1500 units.[29]

On the next page we have another possible Cameron in a poorly done tintype with two ladies with slanted hats doing a jaunty pose with an umbrella.

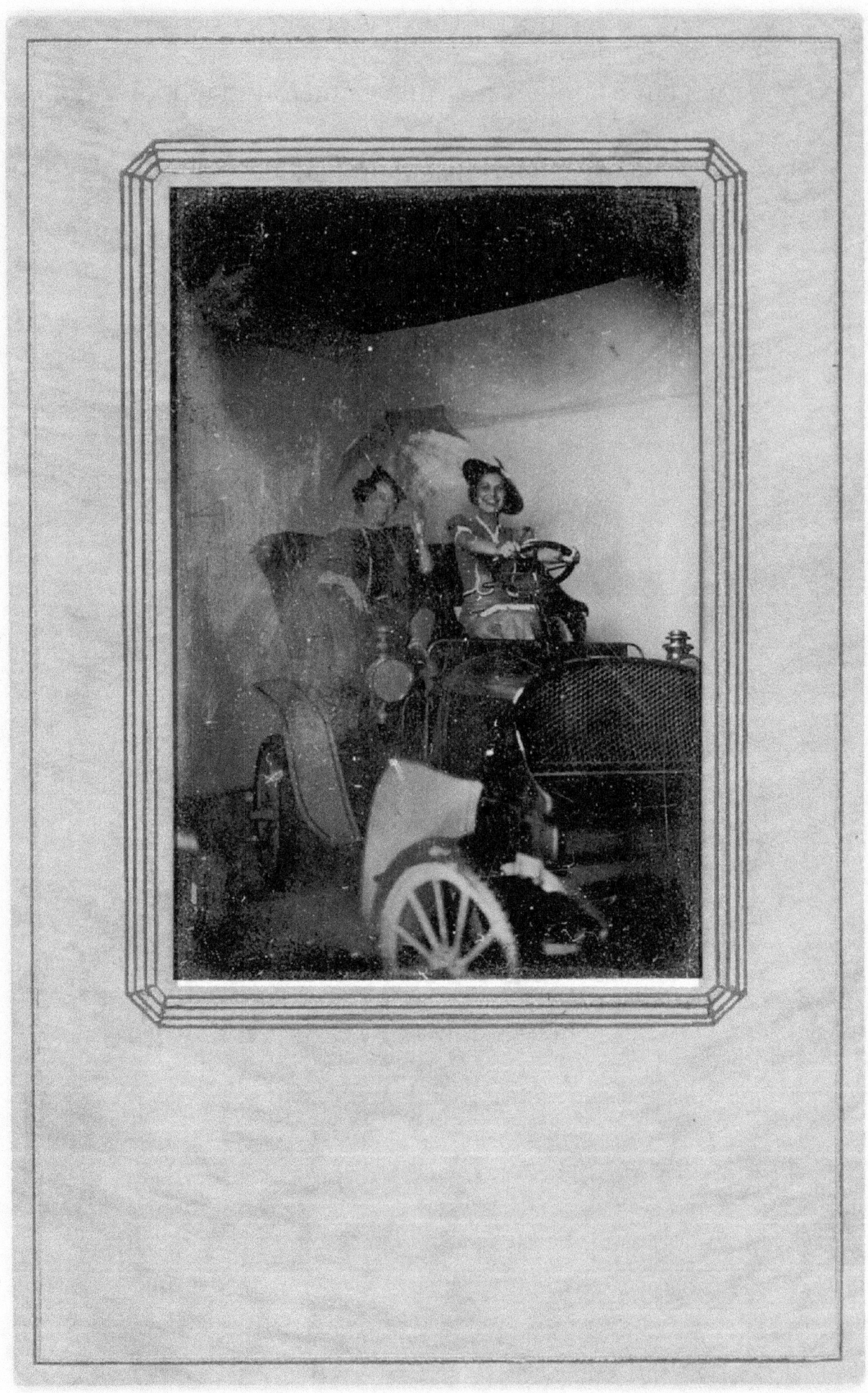

We don't see many other cars on the road so we wave when we see a father and his son posing in a Maxwell 1908 runabout. This is easy to identify because of the sign.

The Maxwell-Briscoe Company of North Tarrytown, New York, manufactured automobiles from about 1904 to 1925. The company was founded by Jonathan Dixon Maxwell who had formally worked for Oldsmobile. His business partner was Benjamin Briscoe, an automobile industry pioneer who was also part owner of the Briscoe Brothers Metalworks. He served as president of Maxwell-Briscoe at its height.

As typical of early automobile companies, it had its ups and downs, moves, and buyouts. In 1907 after a fire destroyed the factory they opened a huge facility in New Castle, Indiana. Newspapers reported that the factory "will operate as a whole, like an integral machine, the raw material going in at one end of the plant and the finished cars out the other end."

For a while, Maxwell was considered one of the top three automobile makers in America, along with General Motors and Ford. Maxwell became part of a combine called United States Motor Company which was formed in 1910. This combine collapsed in 1913 leaving

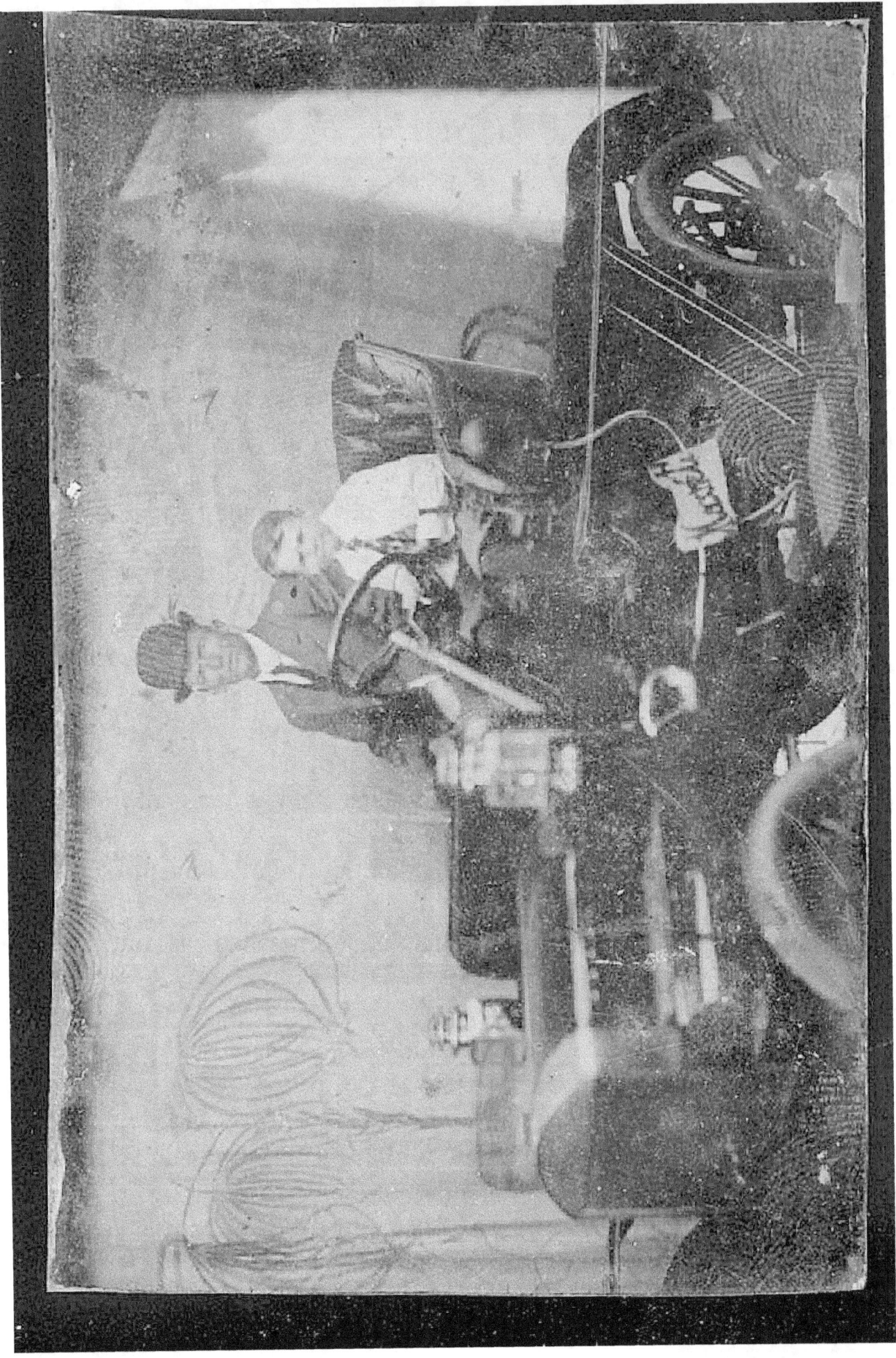

Maxwell the only survivor. In 1913, Walter Flanders, took the wheel reorganizing the company as a corporation. Far in the future, the company was taken over by Chrysler.

Maxwell has the distinction of being one of the first car companies to market specifically to women. In 1909, as a publicity stunt, it sponsored Alice Huyler Ramsey, an early advocate of women drivers, as the first woman to drive coast-to-coast across the United States. By 1914, the company had associated itself with the women's rights movement by hiring as many male sales personnel as female. In another publicity stunt, a woman in a showroom window assembled and disassembled a Maxwell engine in front of spectators.[30]

Early models were two-cylinder with oak frames and body steel that came straight down and wrapped around the oak frame. Maxwell gave up on the oak frame quite early in 1905 because it was weak for the roads of the time. This was changed to a pressed steel frame.[31]

I could only find specs for the Model L, not the one in the picture. It had an eight / twelve horsepower L-head two-cylinder engine with two-speed planetary transmission. It had a solid front axle and live rear axle with semi-elliptic leaf springs, as well as two-wheel mechanical brakes. The wheelbase: was seventy-two inches.[32]

We pass another car. We're unable to identify this one. It could be one of the numerous one-offs or from a short run from an automaker lost to history. The rear wheels are missing and the car is on blocks and has a step placed next to it. It looks like it could even be a buggy with a steering wheel fitted to it. My guess is that is an electric car that dates to before or around 1905. A woman in the Facebook group Ancestry Dating Old Photos named Marjorie said, "Steering wheels began in mid 1890s but most electric runabouts did not have steering wheels until 1901-03. Before that they used a tiller. By 1904 most were using a wheel." Someone suggested that the hats worn pushed back was a style. I think it was done for the photograph. The guy at the wheel looks more like he is actually driving than in most of these pictures where most people either just pose or one might might have hands on the wheel in a half-hearted gesture.

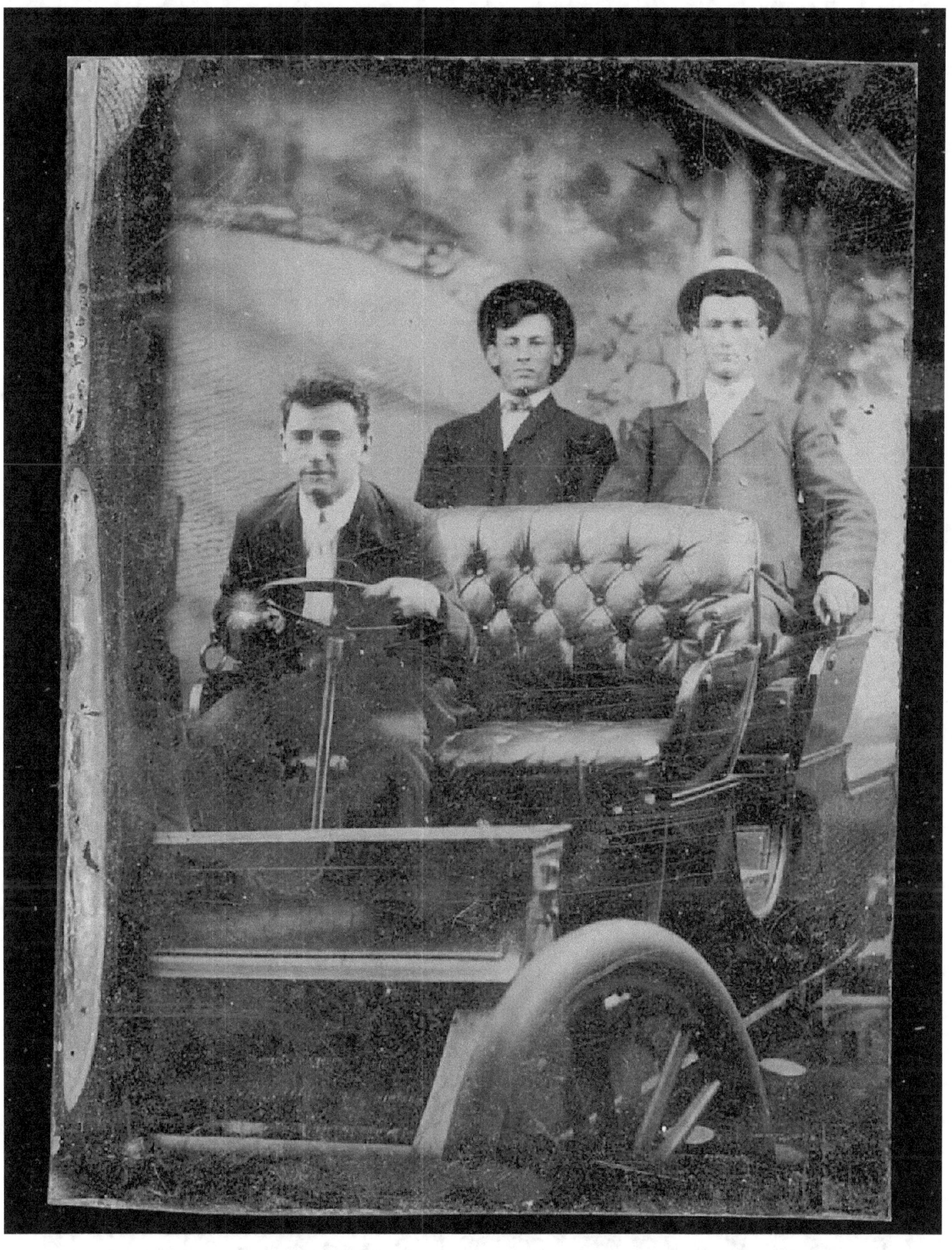

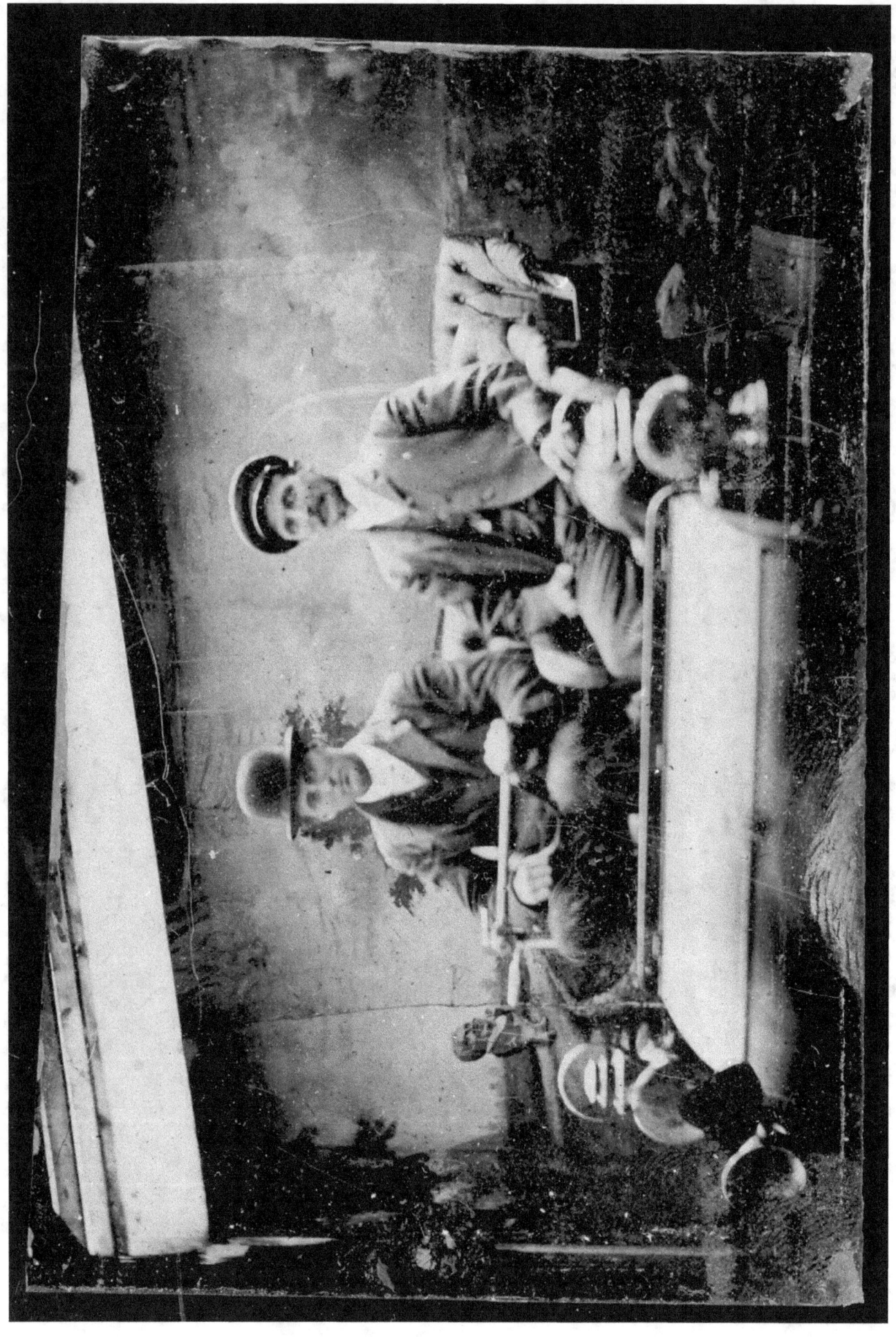

On the previous page is a picture of two men in an unidentified car with a tiller mounted from the side clearly visible.

The next picture shows two guys having fun in what looks like a 1902 Waltomobile Tonneau. It had a 2-cylinder Engine with 12 Horsepower. The manufacturer American Chocolate Machinery Co., which later became Walter, was an American vending machine company in Manhattan that lasted from 1902 to 1906. The company was owned by William Walter. He decided to expand his business by producing automobiles. His cars were exhibited at the New York automobile show.[33]

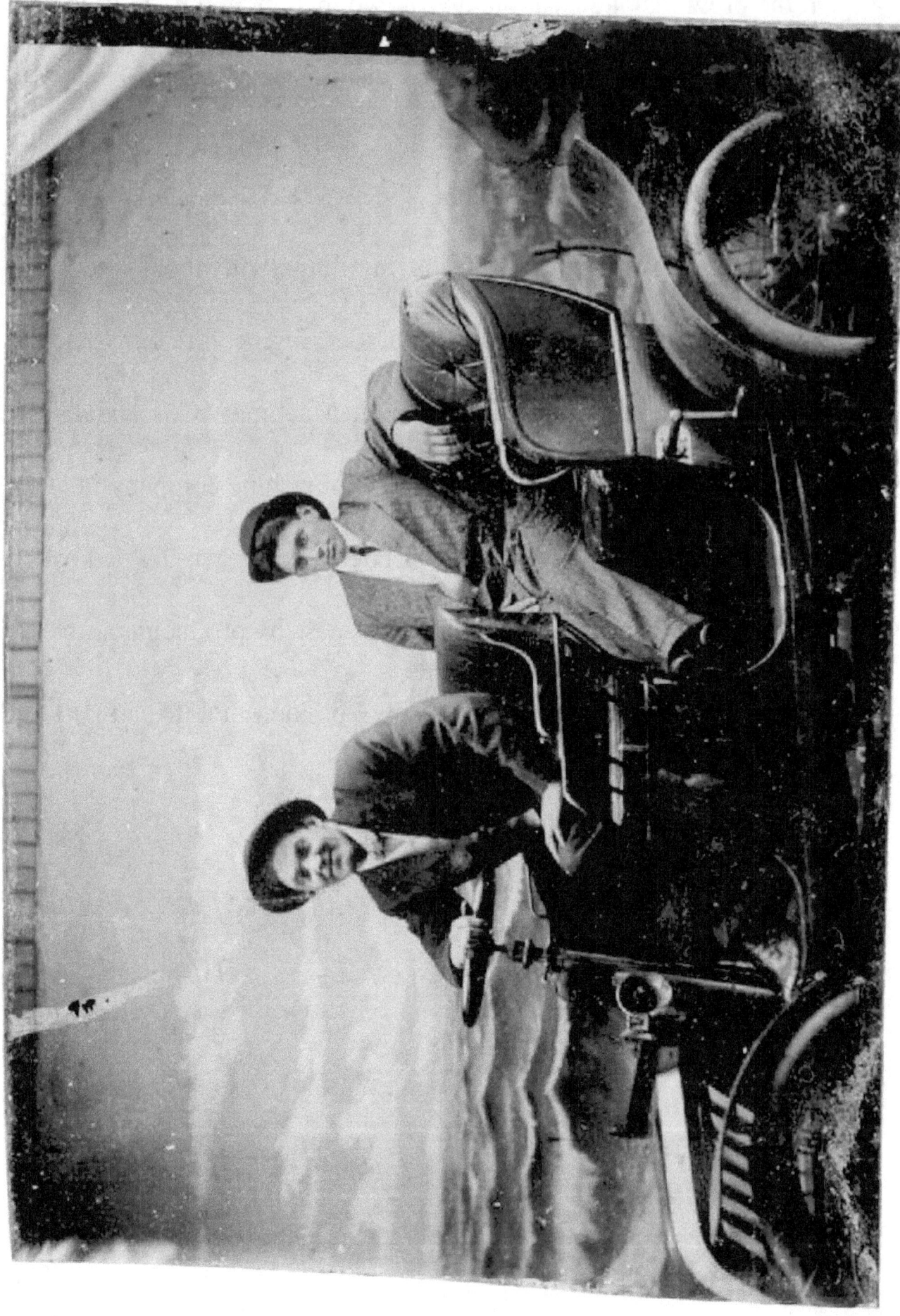

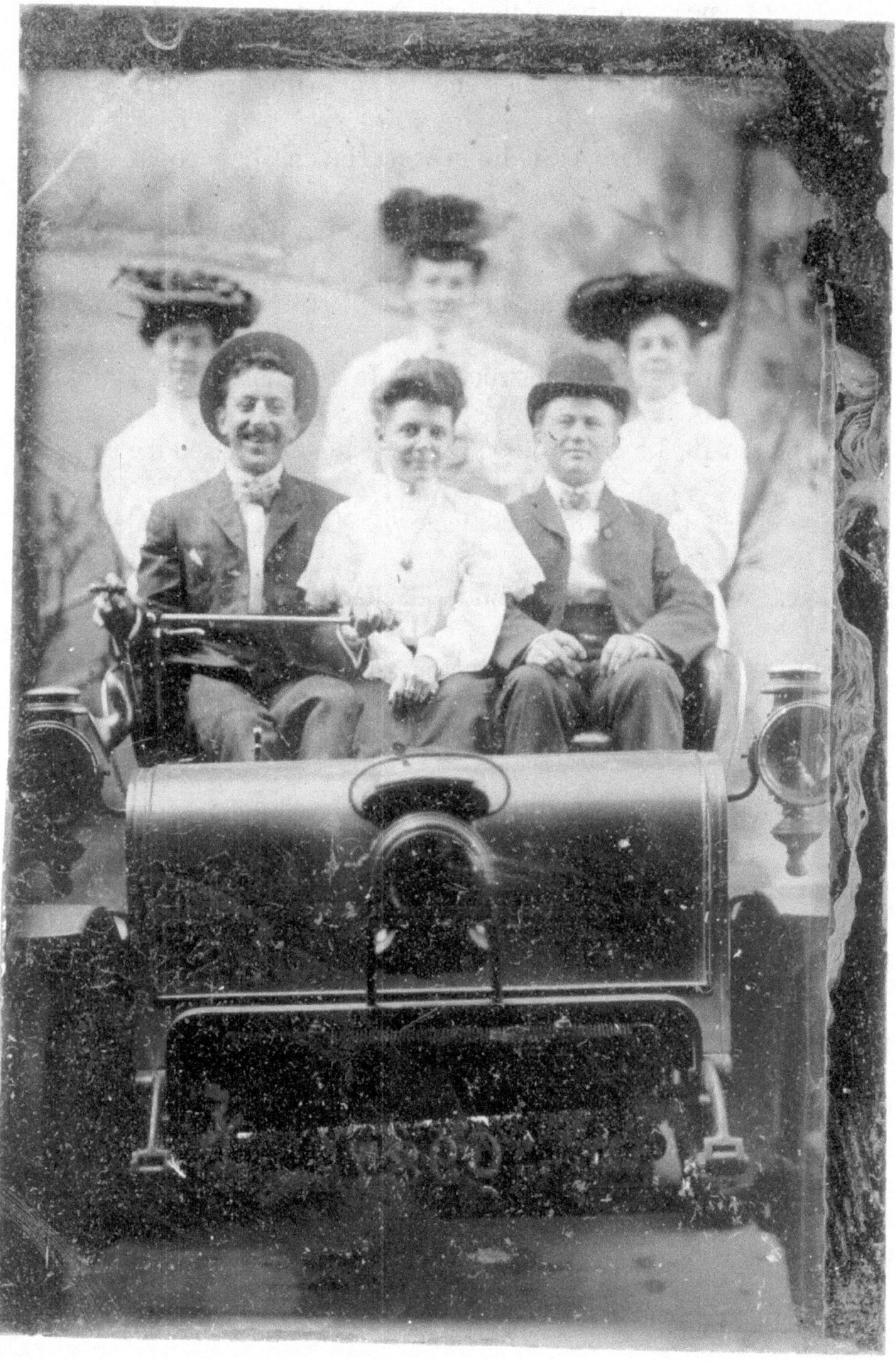

The tintype on the previous page is of six people crammed into an unidentified car with a tiller. This and the photo on the next page was taken at Savin Rock Grove Studio in West Haven Connecticut.

This is a sixth plate tintype of six Ladies in what looks like a 1904 Packard Model L Touring Car was taken C. 1919.

James Ward Packard constructed his first car in Warren, Ohio, in 1899. Then in 1903 a group of Detroit investors purchased the company and moved the operation to a new factory in Detroit. The Model L touring car was the first four-cylinder Packard and the first with the tombstone-shaped radiator shell that became a Packard trademark. The consumer had three choices: a runabout, a surrey, or a tonneau. The body was made of aluminum and wood. The engine was formed from a cast-iron block. The standard paint scheme for the Model L was Richelieu blue for the body with black moldings and cream-yellow striping.

The Model L came standard with two side oil lamps, a rear oil lamp, bulb horn with a tube, tool kit, and storm aprons in both the front and the rear. Optional equipment available; headlamps, wicker side baskets, and sight feed oil gauge.

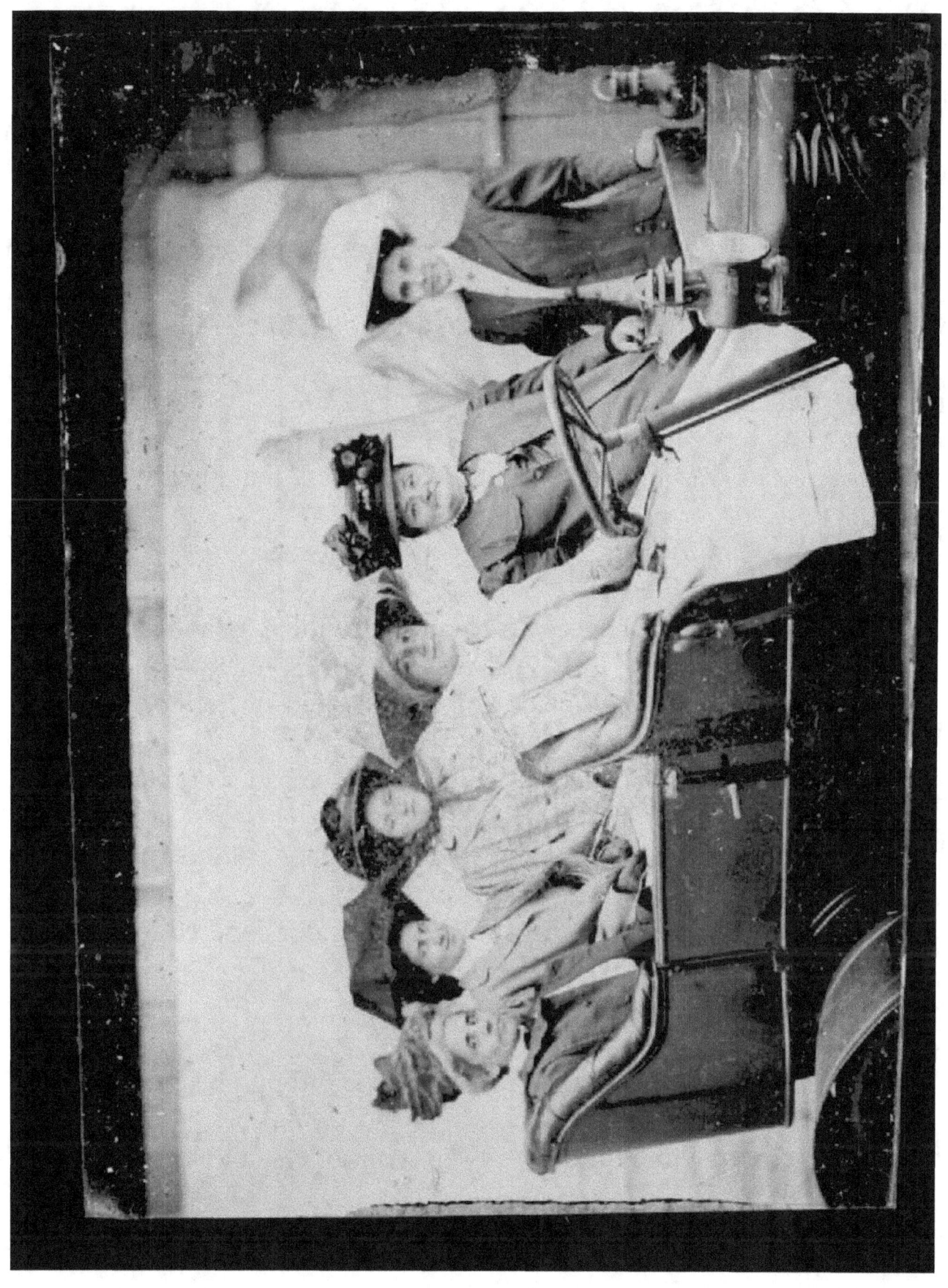

The car's dimensions were – Width: 74 in, Height: 94 in, Wheelbase: 94 in, Length: 147 in, Weight: 1900 lbs, Engine: inline-4, L-head valves,

242 cubic inches. Transmission: 3-speed manual sliding gear transmission with a bevel gear differential and mechanical brakes on the rear wheels. Horsepower: 22 at 900 revolutions per minute, pounds per horsepower: 86.4. The average wage in 1904 was $490 per year. A person would have to work for about 6 years and 1 month to buy this car. In 1904, Packard produced over 200 units.[34]

Savin Rock was an American amusement park that included carousel rides, bumper cars, and numerous fun houses.

The Noah's Ark funhouse was decorated with Noah and his family on the deck, when you went inside you encountered shaker boards and startling animal stunts. The Death Valley funhouse had a skull and cross bone facade which was later replaced with a Laffing Sal. Inside you walked over a swinging bridge, a stretch of the floor covered by a pillow, and a tilted room.

You entered and exited Bluebeard's Castle through his mouth. This funhouse included two tilt rooms, a floor with rollers, and lots of air holes. Plywood cutouts of Bluebeard and his gang startled you with stunts.

The park also featured many roller coasters: The Sky Blazer, The

Racer, The Whirlwind Racer, The White City Flyer, The Devil, and The Thunderbolt. It also had water chutes, one of these was the Shoot-the-Chutes, later rebuilt and renamed The Mill Chutes which featured a moving stairway saving ride-goers a hike to the ride entrance. The oldest ride was The Old Mill, built in 1904. Among the other rides were the Jitterbug, The Virginia Reel, and The Seaplane Swing.

The amusement park originally called White City was established in the 1870s after an entrepreneur named George Kelsey extended the trolley lines and built Liberty Pier at the end of Beach Street to serve as a ferry landing. Kelsey also built a hotel nearby called the Seaview Hotel. This attracted further development of a beachside resort that had a bandstand, a fountain, an observatory, a wooded area for picnics, and a carousel. Amusements were built by other businessmen, a zoo, a museum, and a dance hall. The venue was used for cockfights, horse races, boxing matches, and concerts.

At its peak, the whole area known as "The Rock" also had theaters, restaurants, and hotels along its mile-long midway. Visitors could enjoy shore dinners with frozen custard or get a split-top hot dog from Jimmie's Restaurant, formerly Jimmie's Hotdog Stand. You could drink

'honeydew,' munch on popcorn, and consult mechanical fortune-tellers or The Laughing Lady."

At this festive place, visitors could even watch an auto race at the adjacent West Haven Speedway or see a movie at The Orpheum Theater.

At its peak, Savin Rock Amusement Park attracted 12 million visitors a year. By the 1960s industrial and residential development had grown up around the park, and it gradually lost popularity and became run down. The finally park closed in 1966. However many artifacts from the amusement park are preserved in the Savin Rock Museum and Learning Center in West Haven.[35]

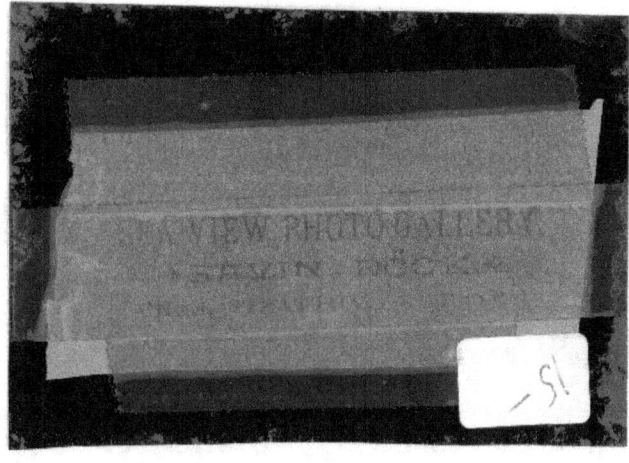

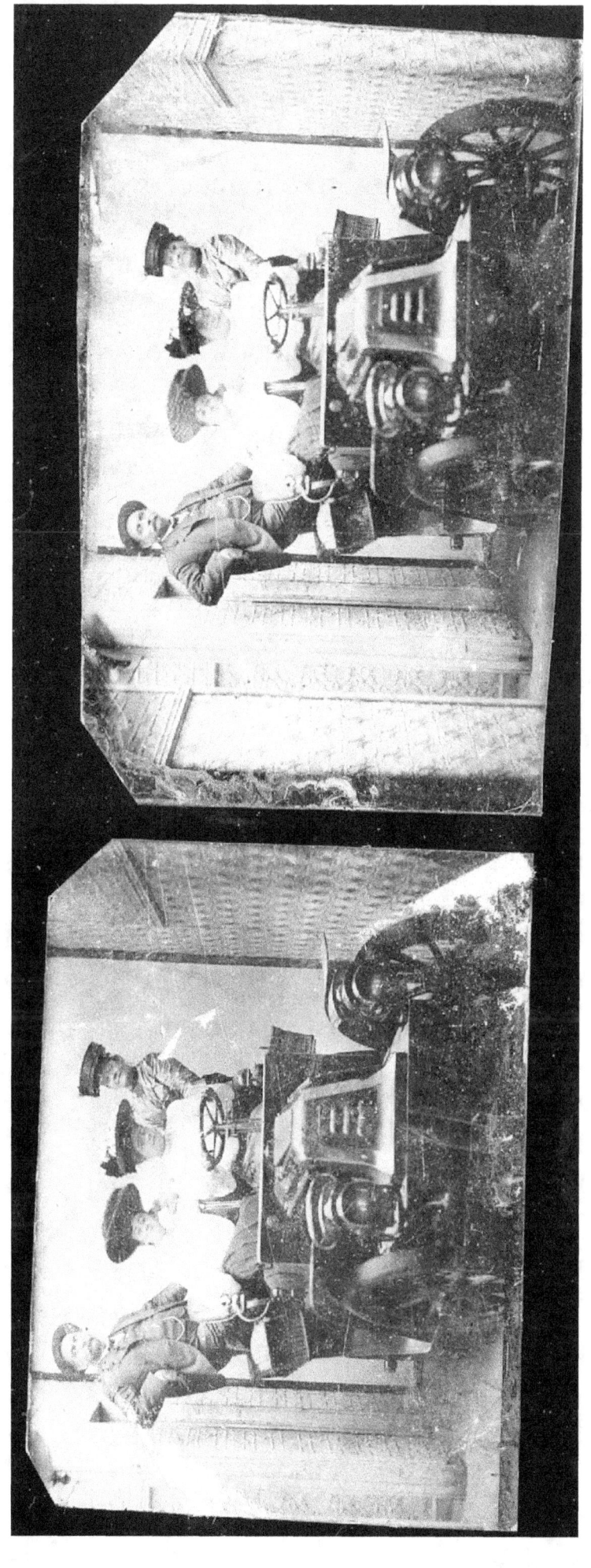

I bought three pairs of tintypes on E-EBay that were shot with a multi lens camera. They were not cut equally to make stereo pairs but when place next to each other and viewed with a stereo viewer they make good 3D images. Except for the four people in an automobile where one picture has paper stuck to it. The guy using a long pole to lean on cracks me up.

This and the next pictue are the same car taken in the same studio. As near as I can figure the car is a Haynes-Apperspon. The Apperson's Riverside Machine Works company was founded by Elwood Haynes and his two brothers Elmer and Edgar Apperson. In 1894, the three of them built one of the first gasoline powered vehicles in America. By 1898 the company was able to produce one new car every two to three weeks. The models sold for $2,000. At the end of that year, they relocated and built a large factory and introduced two additional models. They expanded and increased their production rate to two or three new cars every year. Businesses thrived, they made five cars in 1898, thirty in 1899, 192 in 1900, and 240 in 1901. In order to increase production they kept the factory open 24 hours a day, and had two shifts of workers.

Haynes-Apperson automobiles had a reputation for "long distance running." The company's cars regularly competed in endurance races. In fact a Haynes-Apperson was among the cars entered in the first automobile race in America, the Chicago Times-Herald race from Chicago and Evanston, Illinois in 1895. The last model they made had a three-speed transmission and was capable of a whopping 24 mph on pneumatic tires.

In 1902, the brothers had turned a large profit from the enterprise and they decided to split up to form their own companies.[36]

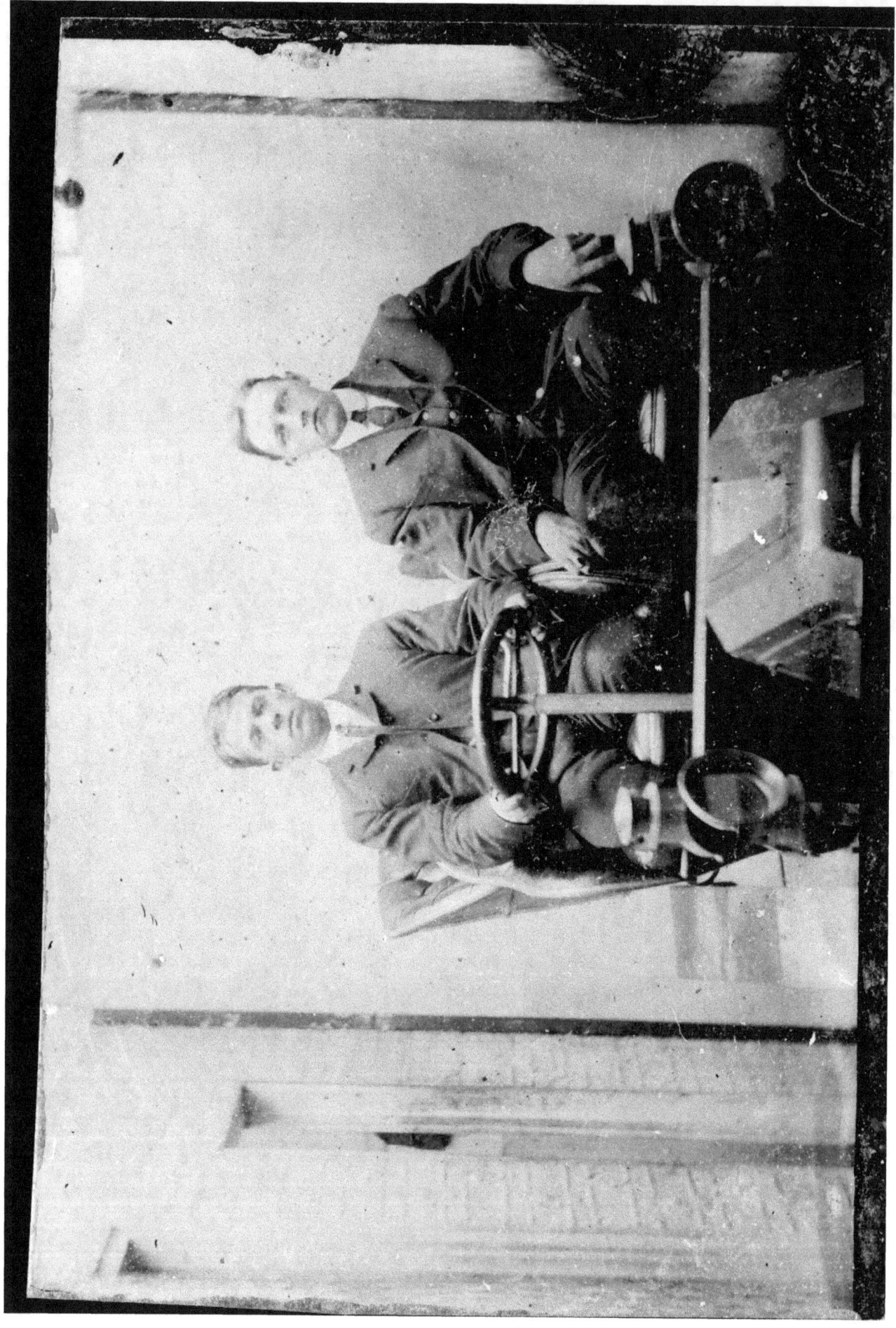

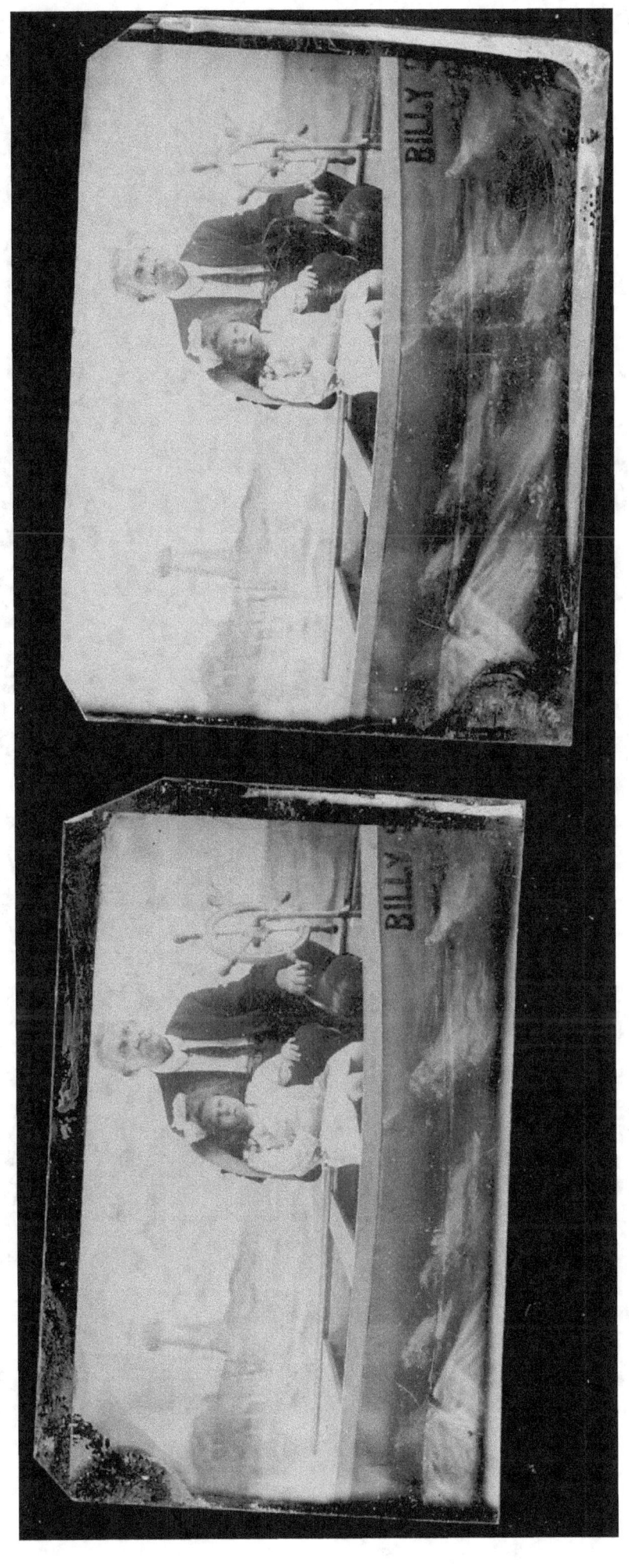

Another kind of vehicle. This is silly having a row boat with a steering wheel. I think it is cool the way the waves are done.

The next picture is the third pair an ordinary group shot.

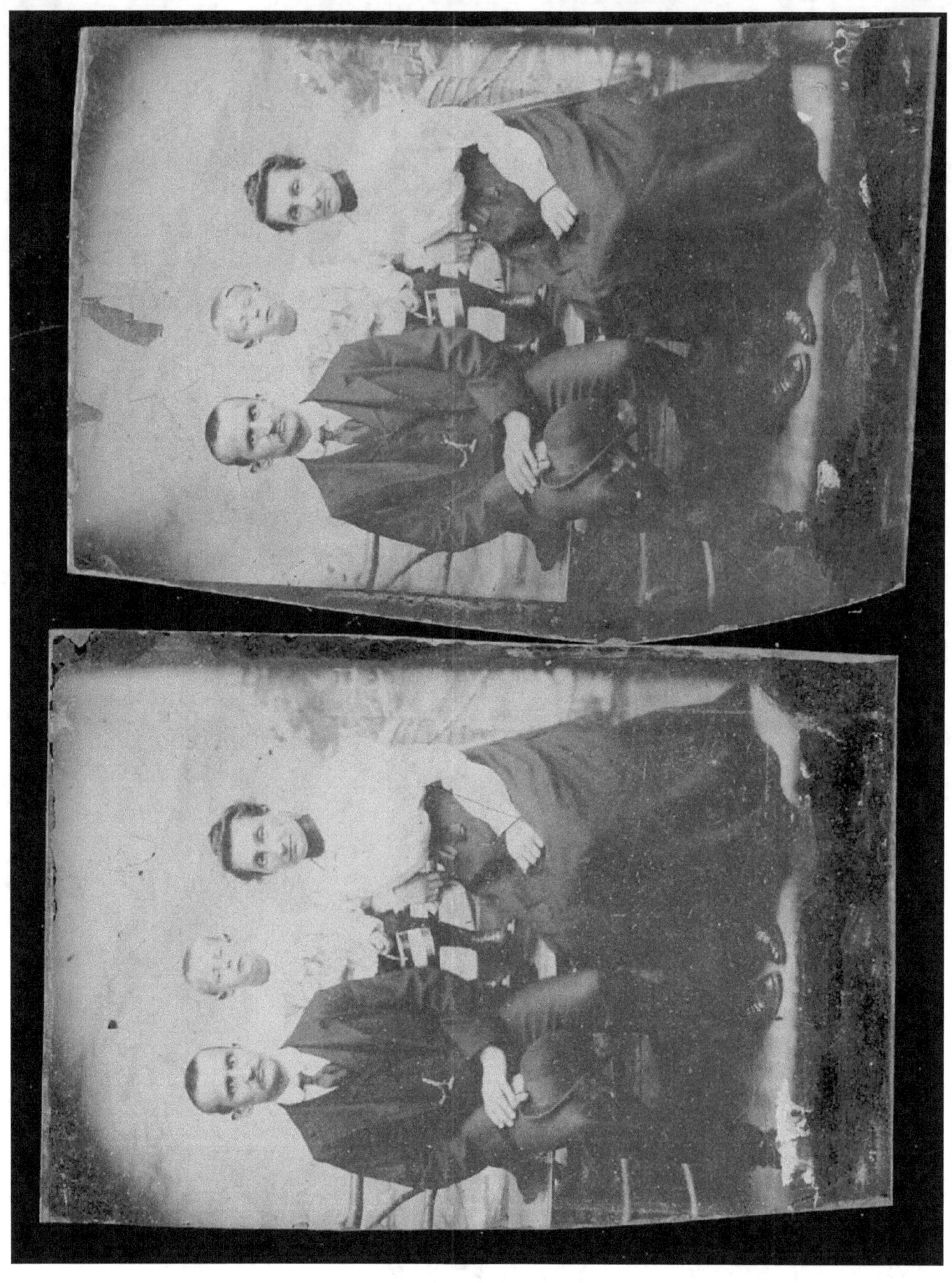

Now we head northward into Maine sometime around 1905 where three friends get their tintype made posing in their best clothes with a newfangled contraption. Sometimes the best images are the more nondescript, poorly photographed, and inexpensive ones. This tintype is one of those jackpot images where I could find out a lot of information. Cynthia Littlefield, guessing from the order of the names, the one on the left, and Olive Mable Ogden both wear plain tailored clothes appropriate for outdoor activities and traveling, topped off with elaborate hats. Olive appears to be dressed in a wool or tweed suit with an ankle-length skirt and matching jacket,[37,38] while Cynthia has a dark wool jacket. Olive's boots have pointed toes and a medium-height heel. They are a leather, laced style[39] appropriate for the outdoors. Walter Makerson wears black lace-up boots suitable for walking in snow and slush that might even be his work shoes. He wears a gray or brown sack coat with matching trousers and a white shirt with pins on the collar with a matching white tie topped off with an ivy cap. The two women are in their late teens. Walter, is in his early twenties.

Cynthia and Canadian-born Walter R Mackerson, board at the house of Albert T Berue in Oldtown Ward 3, Penobscot, Maine on Elm Street.

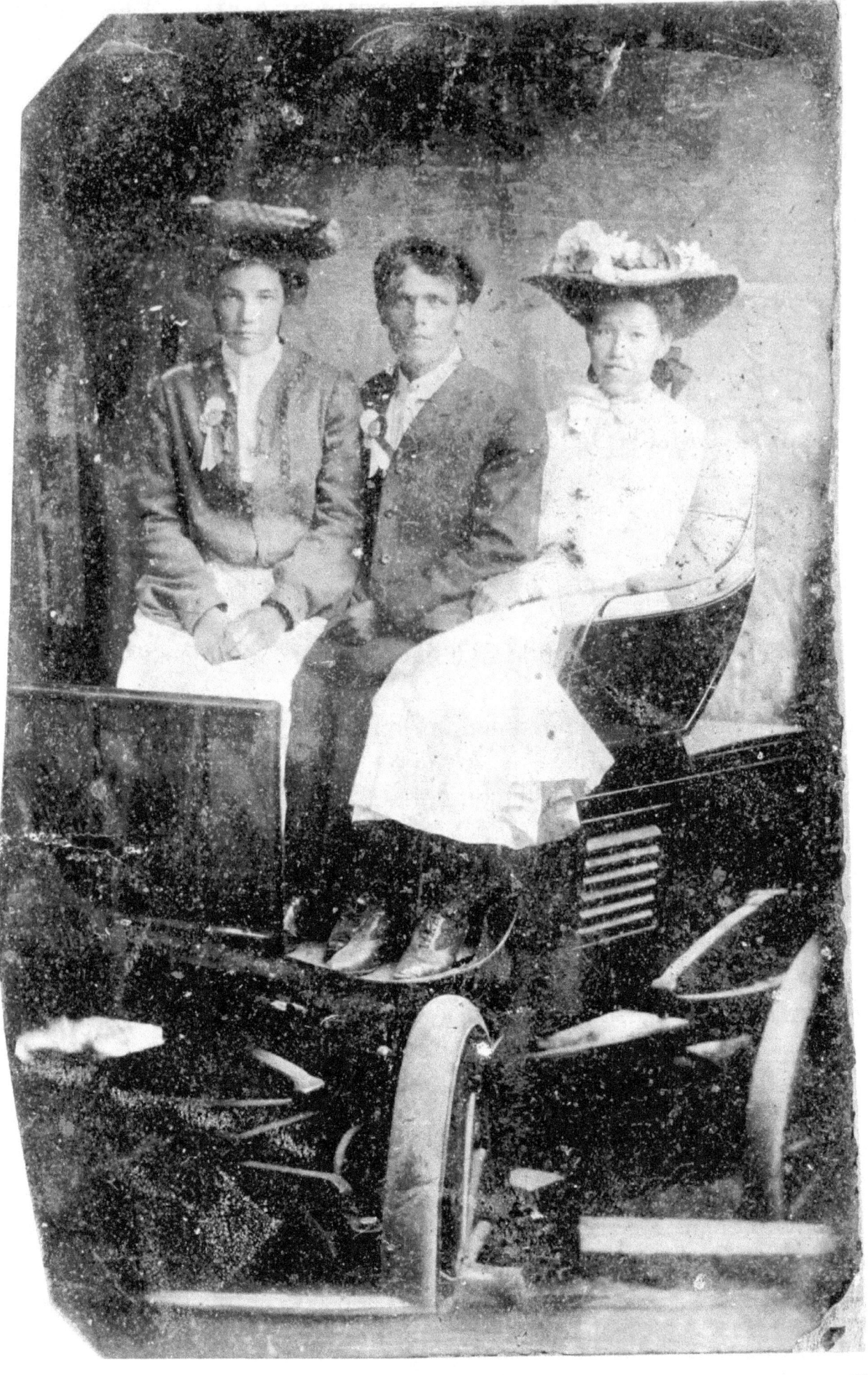

Both work at "The Snow Shoe Factory." Cynthia is a "Tiller" and Walter is a Woodworker. Olive also lives in Oldtown and she too probably works at the factory. All three have a ribbon pinned on them which might indicate that they are attending a convention, maybe in Portland, perhaps having to do with their trade. The car might be a prop for attendees to have their pictures taken in. The Automobile might be another Haynes-Apperson 1899 or 1900 model. These automobiles were equipped with a double-cylinder gasoline engine. The two-passenger Phaetons sold for $1230.00."[40] There is a step placed beside the car to help patrons get in and it appears that the steering apparatus (A different kind of tiller) has been removed as it is bulky and would have gotten in the way.

The other people in Berue home are Albert's wife Myrtie F, his sons Aubrey, and Merle L., his daughters Pearl, Glenys W., Gretal W., and Fern L. The paper that came with the tintype has the name Nickerson on it, but the fact that a woman named Cynthia Littlefield is listed with a man named Walter whose last name is similar is too much of a coincidence. This has to be them and I can distinguish this Cynthia from another woman with the same name. I thought they were the same person at first, but I doubt she lived in two different places. I'm pretty certain I found the right Olive because there are no others in the same period in Penobscot.

Native Americans in Maine made snowshoes not only for their own use for winter hunting and gathering, but also for sportsmen, lumbermen, and recreational snowshoers.

Maine was the center of snowshoe production from the 1850s to the 1940s and Native American snowshoes were renowned for their superb craftsmanship and durability. But snowshoes were not just made by native Americans which brings us back to the people in the tintype who don't look like Native Americans except perhaps Walter. Americans borrowed (or should we say stole) traditional Native American designs and construction techniques. The best known of these were A. M. "Mellie" Dunham, who had a brief career playing the fiddle after he played for Henry Ford.[41] and W.F. Tubbs of Norway, Maine.[42] Tubbs Snowshoe Company was founded in 1906. Tubbs produced high-quality ash snowshoes, skis, sleds, and furniture, even supplying Byrd and Peary's polar expeditions.[43] Penobscot is not close to Norway so "The

Snowshoe Factory" Where the trio worked must have been some competitor or a branch location.

The process of making snowshoes involved getting two pieces of straight-grain, mostly knot-free tree trunks, possibly paper birch, or black ash, which bends extremely well.

Perhaps Walter's job was to split the wood along the grain with wedges and mallet and a froe. (an L-shaped tool, used by hammering one edge of its blade into the end of a piece of wood in the direction of the grain)[44], maintaining the wood grain, rather than sawing across it to create a stronger piece of wood that is less likely to crack. Then he would have shaped the staves down to size around a half-inch wide and three-quarter inches tall. Then he would bend the staves in the form. Next, he soaked the staves in hot water then quickly bent them into place on a form. Afterward, he would do the final shaping and smoothing. Then it was time to mortise (cut a hole or recess into a part which is designed to receive a corresponding projection - a tenon - on another part to join or lock the parts together)[45] for the cross pieces, cutting out the cross pieces, and riveting the ends together.

Now it is ready for weaving the webbing pattern and creating foot bindings. Perhaps this is what the Tiller's job was.[46] Or maybe a Tiller handled money, as in a "till" used by cashiers. Interestingly, there is an instrument used for making shoes that is called a Left Hand Tiller Shoe Kit.[47]

Whether Walter was romantically involved with either Cynthia or Olive is not known. I have a fancy for Cynthia but Olive looks like she might be the wittiest. Walter has more body contact with Olive and Cynthia has to pose awkwardly as the third person in a two-seater, yet she is more color-coordinated with Walter. Well in any case Walter looks like he might punch me if I made a move on either of the girls.

Olive Mabel Ogden married a man named George Oliver Webster on 18 April 1910 in Old Town, Penobscot, Maine.[48] She was born on 26 May 1890 in Passadumkeag, Maine, to George W. Ogden and Henrietta Perrin Pearise.[49] She had a son on 30 Apr 1917.[50] A daughter died 22 Mar 1919.[51] Mazie B Webster was born May 4, 1921.[52] Another Daughter, Mrs. Audrey E Faulkner died 22 January 1998.[53]

There is no other record of Walter or Cynthia. I doubt this is the same Walter M. who worked as a messenger in New Orleans later; he could have been Walter's son. Maybe he moved back to Canada with Cynthia.

On the next page is a photo of two women in an unidentified car with hats that look like they could be used to carry things. I bought it just because I liked it.

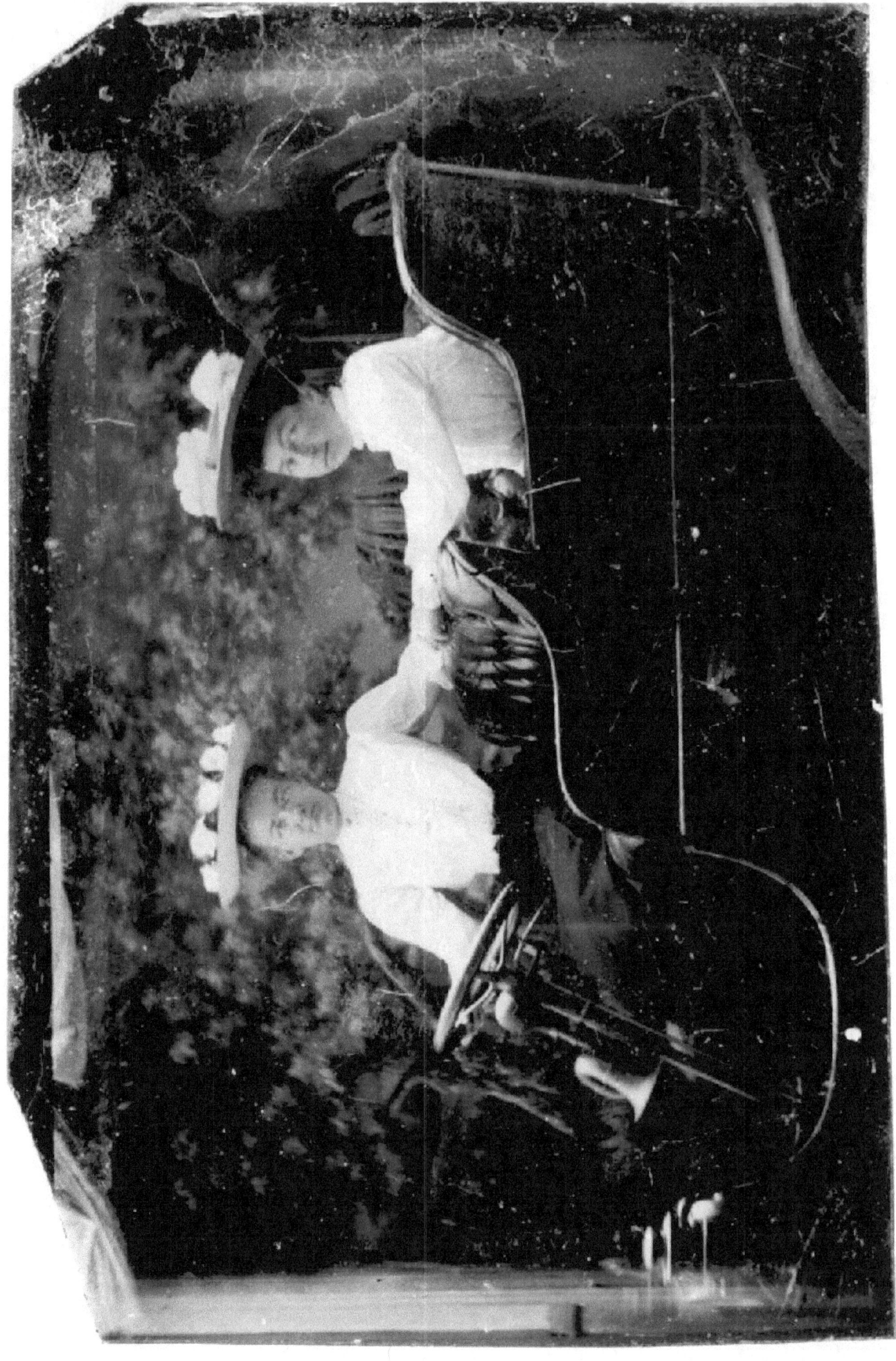

One more stop before this road trip comes to an end. Here we have a 6th Plate tintype taken by a bad photographer of two women and a little girl in a car that is probably a 1905 Cameron Runabout. Not only did the tintypist not varnish the plate so that it wouldn't turn dark, but the little girl's head gets cut off on the edge of the picture and gets further obscured by the paper frame that originally held the image. Here we see why we call the compartment in the back of an automobile a trunk.

The Cameron Company, founded by Everett S. Cameron, started out as a bicycle repair business and then in 1899 made a steam car. After a few years, they got better financial backing and moved to a large plant where they made internal combustion, one cylinder, air-cooled cars. They later expanded into trucks, tractors, and boats. In 1904 they added two- and three-cylinder cars to their lineup, later increasing to four and six-cylinders.

The 1905 Cameron Runabout Ranged in price from $650 to $1,050. The company constantly relocated and was bought several times while making cars from 1903 through 1914. "For 1914, the Cameron Company had hefty goals which were cut short due to World War I and a lack of financial backing. As a result, the company entered bankruptcy." In 1916,

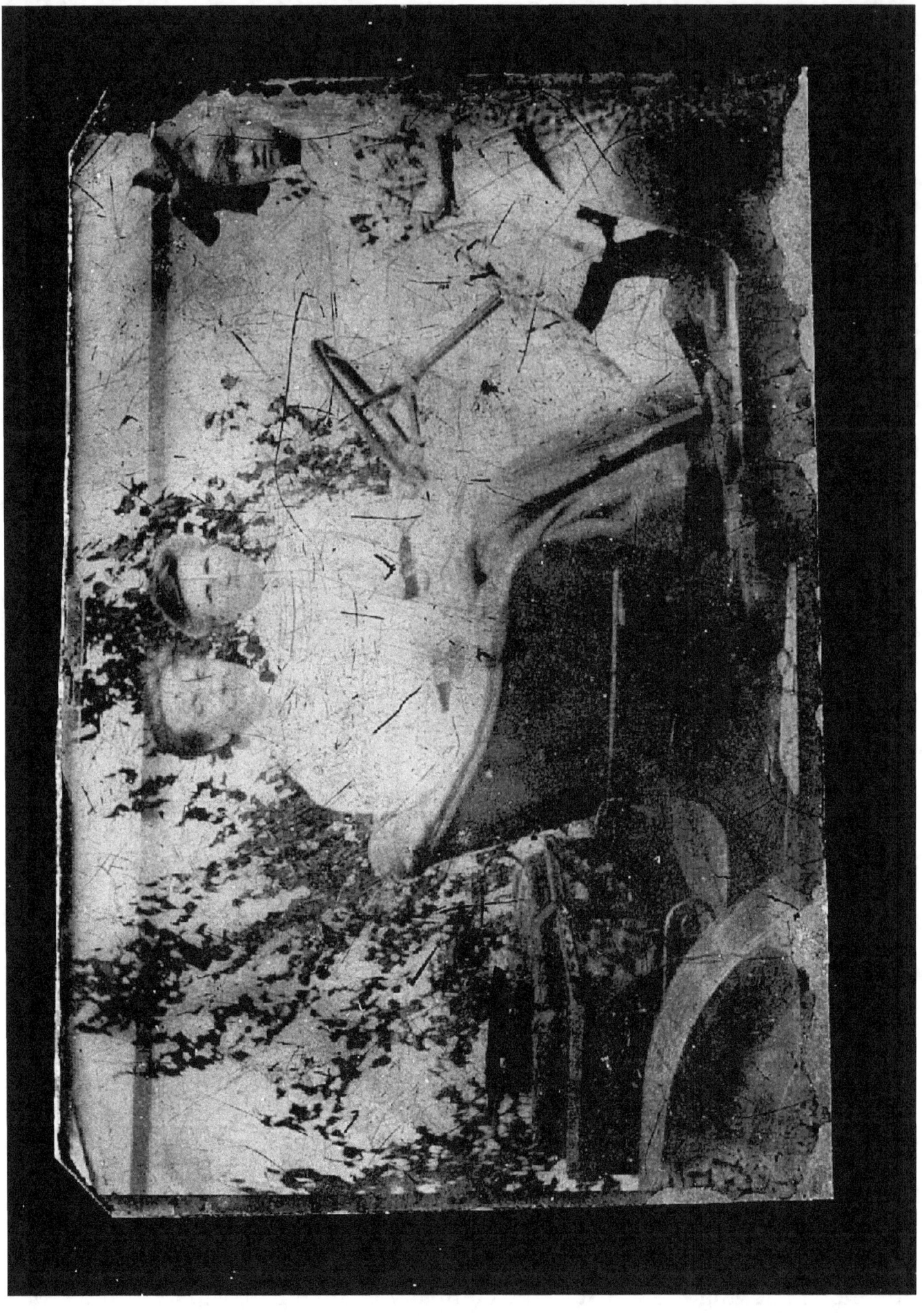

the Cameron Company was briefly resurrected. After a few prototypes were built, the company closed only to have another re-birth in 1919 in yet another factory and petered on through 1920. Their rear-mounted gearbox was revolutionary at the time but fell into automotive footnote history. However, some of their innovations became industry standards, torque tube drive, left-side steering wheels, front-mounted engines, and air cooling. But due to the confusion of the early automobile era cars which came out faster than patents, it is hard to answer Abbot and Costello's paraphrased universal question 'Whose was first?'

"Several Cameron's were used in competition, including hill climbs and dirt track events. One car even captured a half-mile world record in Cincinnati, Ohio. Another vehicle became the first air-cooled car to reach the top of Mount Washington without requiring a stop."[54]

Now we arrive at the garage contemplating that there may be forgotten automobiles by forgotten makers that are only known to history by their image in a tintype taken for amusement. I am unaware of anyone else who specializes in collecting car tintypes and I cannot see or buy everything. It would be nice if enough images could get cataloged and analyzed so that some conclusions could be formed such as whether certain cars were used more than others. Perhaps these pictures are not quite old enough yet to generate interest, or few people take them seriously because of tintype's reputation as a rugged cheap mass-produced medium done by hack photographers to earn a buck.

Yet those qualities are the very thing that I think is cool about tintypes The subjects "liked it best when they could be themselves, straightforward, awkward, and sometimes silly... But at the end of the day, the stories were real, untouched by the manipulations of artist or photographer."[55] Because of the frivolous nature of the way they were taken historically interesting details got inadvertently recorded that might otherwise have been lost.

One more photo. This arrived in the mail as this book was being prepared for publication. We have two women friends each pretty in a different way in exquisite dresses. An amazon with a lively companion. I'm smitten with the girl holding the wheel, but I imagine if I talked to them then the big girl would turn out to be the more personable.

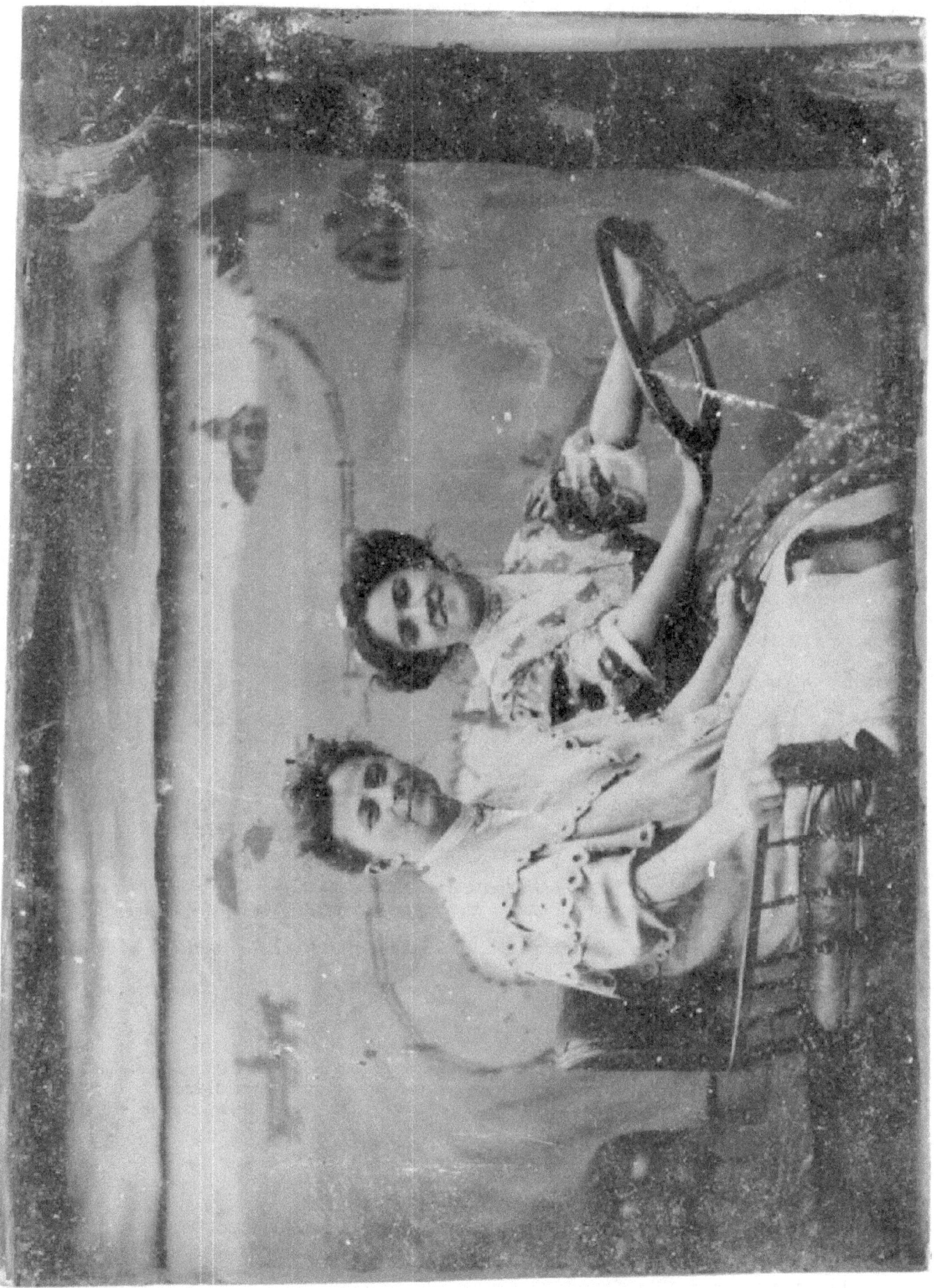

1. Gary W. Clark, Cased Images and Tintypes, Kwick Guide, PhotoTree.com 2013. P 72.
2. Janice G. Schimmelman, The Tintype In America 1856-1880. American Philosophical Society, Philifelphia, 2007. P 1.
3. Ibid, Clark P. 72.
4. Naomi Rosenblum, A World History of Photography, Abbeville Press, New York 1984 P. 196
5. Anthony Hamber, "Photography and the 1851 Great Exhibition. New Castle, Delaware And London, 2018. Dust Jacket.
6. https://www.britannica.com/technology/tintype.
7. https://www.aoghs.org/transportation/first-auto-show/
8. https://en.wikipedia.org/wiki/Steam_car
9. E-mail correspondence.
10. https://en.wikipedia.org/wiki/History_of_the_automobile
11. Gary W. Clark, Cased Images & Tintypes Kwick Guide.PhotoTree.com, 2013. P. 72.
12. The Murphy Automobile Museum. http://www.murphyautomuseum.org/1903-Oldsmobile.html
13 "United States Census, 1910," database with images, *FamilySearch* (https://familysearch.org/ark:/61903/1:1:MPBY-WV1 : accessed 8 November 2020), Willie Cobey in household of Mike Cobey, Alexandria Bay, Jefferson, New York, United States; citing enumeration district (ED) ED 4, sheet 6A, family 128, NARA microfilm publication T624 (Washington D.C.: National Archives and Records Administration, 1982), roll 953; FHL microfilm 1,374,966.
14. https://frenchhatchingcat.wordpress.com/
15. https:/bklyn.newspapers.com/clip/43463627/the-brooklyn-daily-eagle/
16. https://en.wikipedia.org/wiki/Pr%C3%A4sident
17. https://en.wikipedia.org/wiki/Cadillac_Runabout_and_Tonneau#Rear_entrance_tonneau.
18. https://en.wikipedia.org/wiki/Rambler_(automobile)
19. https://www.conceptcarz.com/vehicle/z10512/rambler-model-c.aspx
20. https://www.earlyamericanautomobiles.com/1900.htm
21. http://www.virtualsteamcarmuseum.org/makers/milwaukee_automobile_company.html
22. https://www.familysearch.org/ark:/61903/1:1:WWNX-DF2M
23. Record Collection: United States, Veterans Administration Master Index, 1917-1940
24. https://www.merriam-webster.com/dictionary/coremaker
25. https://www.libraryweb.org/rochcitydir/images/1906/1906u-z.pdf
26. Georgano, G. N., *Encyclopedia of American Automobile*, (New York, E. P. Dutton & Co., 1968), p. 134.
27. http://www.virtualsteamcarmuseum.org/makers/milwaukee_automobile_company.html
28. https://en.m.wikipedia.org/Cliff_House,_San_Francisco
29. https://www.conceptcarz.com/z20928/franklin-model-a.aspx
30. https://en.wikipedia.org/wiki/Maxwell_automobile
31. https://forums.aaca.org/topic/75435-1905-maxwell/
32. http://www.finecars.cc/en/detail/car/97436/index.html
33. https://en.wikipedia.org/wiki/American_Chocolate
34. *By Daniel Vaughan | Oct 201. https://www.conceptcarz.com/z20492/packard-model-l.aspx*
35. *https://en.wikipedia.org/wiki/Savin_Rock_Amusement_Park*
36. https://en.wikipedia.org/wiki/Haynes-Apperson
37.. Evolution of Women's Fashion During the Progressive Era Examined in DAR Museum Exhibition. (16 July 2014). Retrieved 17 April 2017, from http://www.dar.org/national-society/media-center/news-releases/evolution-womens-fashion-during-progressive-era-examined
38. Tierney, T. (2017). Appropriation, articulation and authentication in acid house: The evolution of women's fashion throughout the early years of the acid house culture. Fashion, Style, & Popular Culture, 4(2), 179. doi:10.1386/fspc.4.2.179_1
39. Payne, Blanche: History of Costume from the Ancient Egyptians to the Twentieth Century, Harper & Row, 1965. No ISBN for this edition; ASIN B0006BMNFS
40. American Automobiles. http://www.american-automobiles.com/Haynes-Apperson.html?fbclid=IwAR2mjjaywmdYfXBsdJ9sqjG6KRNdh9VoRbssgEcu0d8pF_ES-ukCXaYxBPc
41. New England Historical Society. https://www.newenglandhistoricalsociety.com/mellie-dunhams-meteoric-rise-stardom/
42. University Of Maine Hudson Museum https://umaine.edu/hudsonmuseum/exhibits/online/snowshoes/maine/
43. Maine League of Historical Societies and Museums (1970). Doris A. Isaacson (ed.). Maine: A Guide 'Down East'. Rockland, Me: Courier-Gazette, Inc. p. 399.
44. https://en.wikipedia.org/wiki/Froe
45. https://www.google.com/search?client=firefox-b-1-d&sxsrf=ALeKk03_DsCIMxWxop7VqPh5KiPm1fABcw%3A1601826568323&ei=CO95X6GvE_HF_Qbp2Y-gCQ&q=mortise&oq=mortise&gs_lcp=CgZwc3ktYWIQARgAMgUIABCxAzIFCAAQsQMyAggAMgIIADIFCAAQsQMyAggAMgUIABCxAzICCAAyAggAMgIIADoECAAQR1CUH1iUH2CLMGgAcAJ4AIABdIgBdJIBAzAuMZgBAKABAqABAaoBB2d3cy13aXrIAQjAAQE&sclient=psy-ab
46. North House Folk School web site. . https://northhouse.org/blog/building-traditional-snowshoes
47. Rural King. America's Farm and Home Store

48. "Maine Vital Records, 1670-1921," database with images, *FamilySearch* (https://familysearch.org/ark:/61903/1:1:Q24J-X9S2 : 13 March 2018), George Oliver Webster and Olive M Ogden, 18 Apr 1910; citing Old Town, Penobscot, Maine, United States, multiple sources, Maine; FHL microfilm.

49. "Maine Vital Records, 1670-1921," database with images, *FamilySearch* (https://familysearch.org/ark:/61903/1:1:2HVG-J64 : 4 April 2020), Olive Mabel Ogden, 26 May 1890; citing Passadumkeag, , Maine, United States, multiple sources, Maine; FHL microfilm.

50. "Maine Vital Records, 1670-1921," database with images, *FamilySearch* (https://familysearch.org/ark:/61903/1:1:Q24J-6DWH : 13 March 2018), MM9.1.1/Q24J-6DWH:, Birth 30 Apr 1917; multiple sources, Maine; FHL microfilm 10,208.

51. Maine Vital Records, 1670-1921," database with images, FamilySearch (https://familysearch.org/ark:/61903/1:1:Q24J-6969 : 13 March 2018), Olive Ogdan in entry for MM9.1.1/Q24J-69DB:, 22 Mar 1919; citing Lincoln, Maine, United States, multiple sources, Maine; FHL microfilm

52. "Maine Vital Records, 1670-1921," database with images, *FamilySearch* (https://familysearch.org/ark:/61903/1:1:Q24J-6K8B : 13 March 2018), Olive M Ogden in entry for Mazie B Webster, Birth 04 May 1921; multiple sources, Maine; FHL microfilm 10,208.

53. "United States, GenealogyBank Obituaries, 1980-2014," database with images, *FamilySearch* (https://familysearch.org/ark:/61903/1:1:QKGL-LTQM : accessed 1 October 2020), Olive Ogden Webster in entry for Mrs Audrey E Faulkner, Maine, United States, 22 Jun 1998; from "Recent Newspaper Obituaries (1977 - Today)," database, *GenealogyBank.com* (http://www.genealogybank.com : 2014); citing *Portland Press Herald*, born-digital text.

54. By Daniel Vaughan | Jun 2013 https://www.conceptcarz.com/vehicle/z9485/cameron-runabout.aspx

55. Janice G. Schimmelman, The Tintype In America 1856-1880. American Philosophical Society, Philifelphia, 2007. P 1.

www.ingramcontent.com/pod-product-compliance
Lightning Source LLC
Chambersburg PA
CBHW082116220526
45472CB00009B/2192